Who Are You?

I DISCOVERED ME FROM A GIRL TO A QUEEN

KAWANIA AMINA BRICKHOUSE

To order additional copies of this book, contact:
Xlibris
1-888-795-4274
www.Xlibris.com
Orders@Xlibris.com

ISBN: Softcover   978-1-7960-9408-4
       Hardcover   978-1-7960-9409-1
       EBook   978-1-7960-9407-7

Print information available on the last page

Rev. date: 03/20/2020

Table of Contents

Introduction

L ord, I want you to be a lamp upon my feet and a light unto my path. My heart pours out, overflowing with thoughts, not knowing where to begin. My soul, my mind, my everything longs to have you near. Where are you? Do you really love me? Do you really care? Do you? These questions constantly rolled around in my head for a long time. I even asked them of my mother, father, sister, brother, girlfriends, boyfriends or *anybody* in sight.

LISTEN TO ME! HOLD ME! Tell me you love this little girl living in a woman's body. The child in me is hungry, starved for attention; longing for what was denied her as an infant after leaving her mother's womb.

***STOP ONE MOMENT! LADIES! ***

If you are pregnant or thinking about conceiving a child, it is vital that you take the life God gives you, cherish it, and pray for that baby with all your heart. It is your offspring, a part of you, and what you do affects the rest of his life. Even what you think about while that baby is in your womb matters. He can hear and feel everything you're experiencing. So cherish the gift of your baby and speak life and loving words over the baby that will soon come. The Bible says, *"Life and death are in the power of the tongue and he who loves it will eat its fruits (Proverbs 18:21).* What you are you speaking over your child?

> *"Whatever is true, whatever is noble, whatever is right, whatever is pure, whatever is lovely, whatever is admirable -if anything is excellent and praise worthy, think about such things. (Philippians 4:8)*

My Testimony

I f I had felt loved and had a blessing declared over me when I was a child, I would not have felt so desperate for attention later as an adult. There were a lot of things missing in my childhood. For one, my conception wasn't planned. Second, my biological father never knew me. I wonder today whether he even knows that I exist. Third, I was an abandoned child, left at nine months old to live with my grandfather and his girlfriend. Understand these are the words of a grown woman typing while the little girl within is crying out desperate for affection. She needs to know that she is loved.

When I cry, pay attention to me. When I'm mad, be mad with me. Yes, I'm the guest of honor at my own pity party. I NEED attention. That's why I did the things I did. For instance, I cried for no reason sometimes. I dyed my hair all sorts of colors or cut it off on a whim then I'd go to the other extreme with long weave trailing down my back. A week later. I would decide to wear my hair natural, sporting an Afro and rocking my roots. Anything for people to stare at me. That was me, Kawania, the odd ball - as a child, all through my teens, and even as a grown woman! That was the old me, the broken me, the desperate, little abandoned girl that longed for attention 24/7.

I was rejected from birth by both mother and father. I was abandoned, sexually abused, confused about my identity as a woman. I was hated, talked about, cursed and surrounded by enemies. The spirit of promiscuity and need for anybody to love me had me bound. I was plagued with infidelity by boyfriends and married a man that did the same thing to me during the entire duration of the marriage. I experienced black eyes and bruised body parts. I have had metal objects thrown at me and was even put in jail twice. I have been through some hard times, but I'm here today to tell the story of a girl that once had low self esteem, thought she was schizophrenic, had no dreams, and bore a child outside of wedlock. All those hurts and offenses broke me, but thank God they didn't kill me. They knocked me down but forced me get up again and try even harder.

I proved that what the world and its statistics said was a lie. Everything I am today is because of what I experienced. It has made me stronger. *"I'm more than a conqueror through him who loves (me) us. For I am convinced that neither death nor life, neither angels nor demons neither the present nor the future, nor any powers, nor anything will be able to separate (me) us from the love of God" (Romans 8:37-39).* My difficulties have been the stepping stone for God to do the impossible in me and through me.

This book is my life story. Every chronicle in here is a testimony of God's saving power and how He took a little depressed child and healed her. I, Kawania Amina, am living up to what my name means. Look at God! Kawania is the name of an island known as a Queensland in Australia. My middle name Amina, was given after an African Queen and warrior who ruled over territory. The enemy had an APB out with my name written on it, but God spoke my name into existence with greatness. He knew I would be a woman of greatness, full of earthly and heavenly riches.

The enemy has the same APB out on you, but guess what? He can't, and he won't, win because God already paid the price for you when He died on the cross and then rose again. We are here for the purpose of being used by God for His glory. I pray whoever reads this book will cry, laugh and most of all, have the courage to write their own life story because it will bring healing to you and others.

> *"Our lives are not our own. We are all born into this world for a purpose and plan"* (1 Corinthians 6:19).

Dedication

THIS BOOK IS FOR:

- the teenager who thinks she has no purpose
- the woman who struggles with rejection and brokenness
- the woman who is considered weird and crazy
- the black sheep of the family
- the woman that never grew up and still has a little girl crying inside of her
- the one that sometimes goes in a closet or in a corner and cries her eyes out until her nose is all stuffed up and she can't breathe well
- the woman who dries her tears, picks herself up, and goes behind her mask

Your mask may be in hiding behind the role of a mother, caught up in tending to your children and their needs. It may be in hiding in the role of a wife keeping herself all dolled up and trying to finish the honey do list. Your mask may be that of a chef lost in making fantastic meals for your family. You may be a professor, cosmetologist, pastor's wife, or even a pastor who everybody counts on to answer their questions or to provide some much needed counseling. Whatever your mask may be, girl, join the club. It's time to take it off and throw it into the 'sea of forgetfulness'.

God loves you and accepts you just the way you are. His Word says in 2 Corinthians 4: 8-10, *"We are hard pressed on every side, but not crushed; perplexed, but not in despair; persecuted, but not abandoned; struck down, but not destroyed. We always carry around in our body the death of Jesus, so that the life of Jesus may be revealed when we are in pain and despair."* You no longer have to remain lost and abused. He paid the price for you and it's time you realize who you are and whose you are. You are the child of the Most High God. You are a Queen and it's time to walk with your head high and chest out believing in the God that lives inside of you.

Every life experience, good or negative, happens for a reason. It all works together for the glory of His name. The strongholds you have struggled with, for half or your entire life, were to develop you into the woman God has called you to be. Remember what the devil meant for bad is turned around for God's goodness.

I would like you to take a moment and write your name out then look up the meaning. Allow God to speak to you about who you are through the meaning of your name. Whether you like the meaning of your name or not. I personally think it can be a positive declaration to encourage you.

_____(Your Name)

meaning of your name_____

My prayer for every person that reads this book is for them to find their true identity and allow God to tear down every area of bondage and family dysfunction that have been carried on for generations. Don't you know there's a reason you have certain habits that you just can't shake? There's a reason you sometimes f ly off the handle in anger when your spouse says the wrong thing to you or your child does something that strikes a core of fear inside of you. There's a reason you can't look at yourself in the mirror and truly say that you love yourself or that you're beautiful. There's a reason you say "yes" to everything somebody asks you to do. There comes a time, though, when you get fed up with pleasing people and not fulfilling what you are supposed to.

Girlfriend, and for the gentlemen reading this book, "Today is your day." This is your time to experience something new. God says it's time to go to the well of water and draw deeper still. He knew that I would write this book and that you would read it. Listen to this: *"He knows the number of hairs on your head" (Luke 12:7)*. Wow, that is awesome!

Our God really cares for us. He remembers something that seems so minute to us but is huge to him. We are His children, His daughters and sons, the love of His life. *"Now devote your heart and soul to seeking the Lord your God. Begin to build the sanctuary for the Lord God, so that you may bring the ark of the covenant of the Lord and sacred articles belonging to God into the temple that will be built for the Name of the Lord" (1 Chronicles 22:19)*.

Be devoted to the Lord our God and stay in His face with prayer, praising, and fasting. He wants to search your soul and tear down every false idol so He can rebuild a new temple in you. He does not desire for you to be perverted with sexual immorality or foul words from music and television shows that corrupt your soul.

I challenge you to try God, seek His face and watch Him do a work in you. *Joshua 1:8 says, "Do not let this Book of Law depart from your mouth; meditate on it day and night so that you may be careful to do everything written in it. Then you will be prosperous and successful."*

Point of Grace, a contemporary Christian group, has a song called "He believes in you". I love this song. It encourages me so much. There's a portion of the song that says, *"When you're at your weakest and hope is still burning through the night but you can't see any rays of hope, You know in your heart that He loves you but in those moments when you can't believe it's true, he believes in you"*. This song is a powerful and dynamic piece for any woman in the world today. The words are saying so much and they are powerful. They describe how dearly our Lord believes in us. He waits patiently for His daughters and sons to come to Him. He waits with open arms and will stay by our side. Now that's POWERFUL. God truly cares for you and He will meet your every need. *"Once I was young, and now I am old. Yet I have never seen the godly abandoned or their children begging for bread" (Psalms 37: 25)*. Hallelujah!!!!! Believe it and receive it this day and for the rest of eternity.

I hope this book will affect your life in a great and dynamic way like never before. Get ready, my darlings, to take the band-aide off the wound that has pained you so long. Isaiah 45:12-13 reads, *"I am the one who made the earth and created people to live on it. With my hands I stretched out the heavens. All the stars are at my command. I will raise up Cyrus (put your name here) to fulfill my righteous purpose, and I will guide his actions. He will restore my city and free my captive people without seeking a reward! I, the Lord of Heaven's Armies have spoken."*

I had to write this book although it has taken seven years to actually complete it. Our lives, my friend, are not our own. They belong to the Lord. Amen! Psalms 37: 23-24 says, *"The Lord directs the steps of the godly. He delights in every detail of their lives. Though they stumble they will never fall, for the Lord holds them by the hand"*

I'm Grateful for:

My son Cincere for being the best photographer ever. I love you and your amazing. To my daughters Uniquek and Vysion and my son Aj, I appreciate you three putting up with my many questions and helping me choose the best pictures and giving me awesome ideas to make this book great success for all. God truly blessed me with 4 wonderful gifts .

I want to thank Rico Sanchez @ Beauty Restoration. My elegant army fatigue blouse and hot red pants were perfect. I had no idea when I purchased my outfit a year ago, I would save it for my book cover.

Mrs. Pat S. Black, I'm so blessed to have you in my life. Thank you for everything.

Finally, I want to thank God for giving me the wisdom and knowledge and creative ability that I know only comes from you. I adore you Abba for believing in me, I'm truly nothing without you.

Purpose

I BELIEVE WOMEN AND MOTHERS HAVE a great purpose. Many, however, are broken and have lost their sense of purpose. I believe it's time to make your life simple by going back to your first love. Fall in love with the Lover of your soul! Begin by being vulnerable. Let your guard down and allow God to rub you where it hurts. He can make it all better. You may have gone through suffering that seems like it will never end but God's Word says, *"Rejoice in our suffering because we know that suffering produces perseverance, character and hope. And hope does not disappoint us, because God has poured out his love into our hearts by the Holy Spirit whom he has given us (Romans 5: 3-5).*

The Holy Spirit is our Comforter. He is our true, true friend. Depend on Him. He will make it better all the way to the end. Let me ask a question. Do you really, really want to be healed? Well, come on! Let's go to the river of living water and face the shadow of death because where death is, God's power can give you life. Stop wondering what, when, where, why and how; just come on and go. Remember what God's Word says in 2 Corinthians 10:5, *"We take captive every thought to make it obedient to Christ".* That's right! Arrest your negative thoughts and tell Satan, "You have got to go. You can't dwell here!"

Ladies, Philippians 4:8 says, *"whatever is true, noble, right, pure, lovely, or admirable; if anything is excellent or praiseworthy, think about such things".* Change those thoughts, girl, and start seeing yourself as a true woman of God with a passion for the things of God. Be on fire for His Kingdom work. Be loving toward your family and friends. Be healed from all abandonment, rejection, self-hatred and doubt. Girl, it's time to pick up your cross like Jesus did and carry it.

Read Philippians 3:10-12, *"I want to know Christ and the power of His resurrection and the fellowship of sharing in His death so that I may attain the resurrection from the dead. Not that I have already obtained all this or have already been made perfect, but I press on to take hold of that for which Christ Jesus took hold of me".* You can do it. It's time to forgive those who hurt you or even to forgive yourself. Whatever it is, God's grace is sufficient for you. It's time to stop living in fear and low self-esteem. Lift your head and walk in confidence that you can be made whole! Let me share the following poem with you:

A CONFIDENT WOMAN

A confident, loving Woman, who can find?????
Jewels and fashion come and go, but a True Woman of God is the best
and one of a kind.
Her worth is not in how she looks on the outside, but her value
is based solely upon Abba Father, Her True Divine.

A confident woman walks with grace, lives with purpose, and can't
wait to see the day she gets to look her King in the face.

A confident woman steps out on faith!
She dares to be challenged by obstacles of life
because her Knight in Shining Armor
will fight the good fight.

A confident woman sparkles like a Diamond, roars like a Lioness, and gathers
her army of Beauty Queens… Not to boast or to be seen,
but to teach them how to stand for pure femininity. To take back what the devil stole… and say it's alright
to be a woman of vulnerability… because that is who we are.

We are confident Women, Loving Women, who seek beautiful love wholeheartedly.
We are Diamonds!

By Kawania Amina Brickhouse

Foreword

INDEED YOU WILL LOVE THIS book as you will read it over and over again. Kawania will have you on a roller coaster of laughter and tears only to drop you off at a sunrise of devotion and inspiration. After unapologetically putting in every thought, life process, and experience, delicate and intentional guidance was carefully crafted in each page. You will find a place of wholeness, discovery, and self admiration. This book will both teach and inspire you to navigate painful emotions, harmful perspectives and experiences that many times have been left unattended to rot into a sea of bitterness. Dare to travel time with us as we journey from infancy to woman hood. This book is recommended to all to mend the broken pieces, clean up and avoid abuse through wholeness and a God like perspective. Next destination... Triumph and Victory. We all could use a little bit of "show me how." Beautifully broken. Kawania you definitely have a gift of helping us all to blossom into our true identity.

Portia Bryant

Kawania Amina Brickhouse is an amazing inspiration in her page turner, *what the devil meant for her bad*. She shares her story in a straight from the heart, down to earth southern style lanced with a sense of humor and bitter honesty. Having weathered many storms, she is a perfect source from which young women can gather strength and courage. Kawania is pulling women out of the chains of generational curses and darkness into freedom and prosperity. Turn each page and see a piece of yourself in her stories. Let God lead you to the well of water…and dare to go deeper still.

Unknown

After reading the pages of this book I felt the compelling need to ask myself "Who Am I"? I felt also the importance of revealing my true inner self with its good and bad. There is an evangelistic part of Kawania's book that reminds me that our God through Christ Jesus is always in control and that in him we are more than the sum of our freshly bodies. And we are more than conquerors though Jesus Christ who strengthens and loves us. Thank you my sister. For you have truly been open from the heart and it has enlightened my soul and spirit. And I know it will do the same for all and I encourage all to read this book in Jesus Name. Amen

Rena Boyd

CHAPTER 1

Who Are You?

THIS WAS THE QUESTION I used to ask myself. After experiencing a lot of Hell on earth: from rejection at birth to molestation as a child to a teen struggling with my identity - being very promiscuous and craving love - to an adult marrying at a young age only to experience more abuse and a failed marriage. I started to wonder, "Lord, why did you make me? Lord, who am I? Why am I here? What is my purpose?" These questions constantly ran through my head. There were even thoughts of suicide. I was so confused. I felt so empty. I needed to discover who I really was.

One day I was introduced to the One who wipes all tears from our eyes. Through His Word, I began to see who I am. It didn't matter what others said, *He* said in I Peter 2:9 *"But you are a chosen people belonging to God, that you may declare the praises of him who called you out of darkness into his wonderful light."* I felt so honored. I had been *chosen*! I was not confined to the titles that once held me captive. They no longer defined me. I am a queen. I am a beautiful creation, made to beautify the world with my creative gifts, talents, and most of all, my presence.

My question for you today is "Who are you?" I challenge you to go on a search and discover the answer. I say to you today that you are royalty... a queen or king made to rule and bless the world with the sweet fragrance God has placed inside of you. God gave me a special passage a year ago. It was presented to me by a beautiful woman of God who I believe is a prophetess to all women. At the time I received it I was desperately looking for answers concerning my life. I was at a small group gathering called *Vision Chaser*. That night God appointed this powerful Word to be spoken over me so that I could have life once again. This same woman is now a dear covenant friend and confidant who encourages me weekly to complete my goals; one of them was to finish this book you are reading. I want to share the passage with you and hope it encourages you as much as it did me:

> *"On the day you were born your cord was not cut, nor were you washed to make you clean, nor were you rubbed with salt or wrapped in cloths. No one looked on you with pity or had compassion enough to do any of these things for you. Rather, you were thrown out into the field. For on the day you were born you were despised. Then I passed by and saw you kicking about in your blood. As you lay there in your blood I said to you "LIVE!" I made you grow like a plant in the field. You grew up and developed and became the most beautiful of jewels. Your breasts were formed and your hair grew; you who were naked and bare.*
>
> *Later I passed by. When I looked at you and saw that you were old enough for love, I spread the corner of my garment over you and covered your nakedness. I gave you my solemn oath and*

entered into a covenant with you, declares the Sovereign Lord, and you became mine. I bathed you with water, washed the blood from you and put ointments on you. I clothed you with an embroidered dress and put leather sandals on you. I dressed you in fine linen and covered you with costly garments. I adorned you with jewelry. I put bracelets on your arms and a necklace around your neck. I put a ring in your nose, earrings on your ears and a beautiful crown on your head. So you were adorned with gold and silver.

Your clothes were of fine linen, costly fabrics and embroidered cloth. Your food was fine flour, honey and olive oil. You became very beautiful and rose to be a QUEEN. Your fame spread among the nations on account of your beauty, because the splendor I had given you made your beauty perfect, declares the Sovereign Lord" (Ezekiel 16:4-14)

This summary is a wonder picture of God rescuing an abandoned baby left out on the street. Your story could be like mine where your birth mother left you and never came back. You might have been put up for adoption, were a victim of abuse, or may have even run away. Whatever your story is, the Lord has a strong love for the fatherless and motherless. Jesus loves you so much. *"Even if my mother and father abandon me the Lord will hold me close" (Psalms 27:10).* He cares about every important thread of your life. You're not a reject; you are accepted by the Beloved. He came to save you and make sure you have the best.

TIME TO RELEASE

So my question to you? Who are you? Don't write down the title of what you do. I want you to truly go within and write out definitions of who you are . We all are unique and have a special purpose and when you discover that, you will fly free like a bird.

Now pick up your pen and release…..

_____

_____

_____

_____

_____

_____

_____

_____

_____

_____

_____

_____

_____

NOTES

NOTES

_____

_____

_____

_____

_____

_____

_____

_____

_____

_____

_____

_____

_____

_____

_____

_____

_____

CHAPTER 2
Given Away Twice

FATHER, MOVE BY YOUR SPIRIT.

I WAS BORN ON JUNE 21ST-- the first day of summer-- in Philadelphia,Pennsylvania. My mother, was supposedly impregnated by one man but recently told me she put another man's name on the birth certificate. While I may not be sure who my birth dad is, I know I have Jesus Christ's DNA f lowing through my veins and that's all that matters.

I am the third oldest of nine siblings. We all have different father's accept two of us, but we all resemble each other. A relative of mine says, "Each person represents a color of the rainbow". Although I have a big family, only three of us grew up in the same home. The others where raised by different family members. That was really a blessing from God because we could have all been given away to foster homes… but for the grace of God. Hallelujah!!!!! My birth mother carried me to term but dropped me off at my grandfather's house when I was nine months old. She asked his girlfriend to watch me for a few hours, but never returned to pick me up. My grandfather raised me until I was five years old. As a result of my abandonment, I was told I had many crying spells. I was taken to the doctor and diagnosed with depression.

I was a very reserved child, but there were a few good memories. I went to Cheeks Pre-Educational Center and can still remember the first word I learned in Spanish-- *uno.* I also remember having birthday parties and playing with the children next door. I especially remember special moments with my grandfather and lying on the bed with him. He always pinched my nose, which was his way of showing affection. What I didn't know at the time was that Grandfather would also leave me.

When I was five years old, he brought me to Virginia and dropped me off at my Relative house (who I eventually called my mother and father). I remember a mini U-Haul packed with all of my stuff, I had assumed we were just going on a trip. The last bit of affection I received from my grandfather was when he pinched my nose for the very last time after dropping me off that day. Why was I left like that? What had I done? I was scared and confused. I remember wondering what would happen next. Who would love me?

My first sign of love came when I went to a room in the back of the house.

Other children were there and a little boy on the top bunk bed smiled at me. Though I did not know him, at that moment I felt so close to him. When he smiled, he eased the pain and fear that imprisoned me. I learned later that he was my sibling who I had never met or didn't remember at the time.

The Spirit of Abandonment and Rejection has been on my family for generations. This cycle actually started back with my grandfather's generation, as far as I know. Grandfather was the youngest of 17 children. His mother died when he was 2 years old and his father was very strict. Sadly, he did not receive any real affection as a child. As a young boy, my grandfather had Rickets, a condition affecting the legs. He even had to have help getting on the school bus until he learned how to walk properly. This made him feel even more shut out from everybody else. Grandfather's father was wealthy and lived in a huge home that had been left to him and siblings. His sibling sold the house out from underneath him, which caused a great wedge between the siblings. This was the beginning of the disconnect.

Grandfather married my Grandma and they had six children together, but he abandoned her for another woman. He was a very abusive man and often beat on my grandma. It was said that he didn't want her but didn't want anyone else to have her. My grandma went to confront grandpa about a situation Where they had a altercation because he had a tendency of putting his hands on grandma. She left to go stay with her brother to get away from the drama. While being there she had complications went to the hospital died and then later the doctors discovered the baby was still alive. My Great Aunt was called and she went to hospital for her last sibling the youngest child. It was rumored that Grandma had been whipped by my grandfather because he didn't believe that the baby was his. As a result, of my Grandma death my aunts and uncles were all split up among different family members.

Grandpa didn't solely beat on my grandma, but just about all his women. He was married three times and lived the rest of his days in Philadelphia where he was diagnosed with Alzheimer's. I went to see him when he was placed in a nursing home, but he could barely remember me. He died alone on November,2004. In his will, he requested to be cremated and left nothing for his children or grandchildren. All we had were his ashes and memories we shared that none of us wanted to bring up.

I told you some of the foundation of my life because I want to let you know how important it is to talk to your children about the history within your family. I believe if you know about your past, you can prevent yourself from going down the wrong path and have a better future. You can begin to renounce spirits that try to attach themselves to your life. If you don't know why you struggle with some addiction or habit you just can't break, maybe it's because your grandma, grandpa, or even great grandparents dealt with these issues. I know you 'Christian' folk say. "Well, why did Jesus die for us then? I thought everything was done away with on the cross?" That's true but it doesn't mean a spirit won't try to pursue you. As long you as live on this earth, you are going to be tested through trials and tribulations.

The Bible says to "*be of good cheer for He has overcome the world,*" (John 16:33). It's important to renounce habits, rituals, addictions and so on from the first, second and third generations. What does that mean? Learn to speak out loud against the negative things you know about your family line and declare they have no hold over your life or your family's life. Declare positive words and the Word of God over your life because the Bible says "*life and death are in the power of the tongue" (Proverbs 18:21).*

Recently, I have had some important intimate conversations with my birth mother that made me realize why I am the way that I am. My mother is not much of a talker but she is very observant. I was on the phone for hours, pulling her teeth, asking questions she probably wouldn't have answered for me otherwise. It was painful but necessary.

Not too long after I left my ex-husband, I had one of those days of feeling lonely and wondering why my life was the way it was. I called my mother in California and we began to talk. We stayed on the phone for about two hours. I asked her what dreams she had in life. To my surprise, her dreams were very much like mine though they never came true. Those intimate conversations with my birth mother helped me realize why I am the way that I am.

My dream to have a family and home did come true for a season... eight years … but the merry –go-round ended in divorce. My point in bringing all this up is to show why you have to get to the root of your issues and pluck them out. My root, my mother's root, and -- maybe your roots -- are planted in rejection and abandonment. Whether it was because of death, a broken mental state, giving up a child, or not being able to raise him, these things have been a silent killer in my family line.

My mother just wanted to be loved. As I told you, her mother died when she was really small. She went from one family member's home to another until she hit her teens. Then her father took her to Philadelphia, which at that time probably wasn't the best decision for my mother. She saw things a young girl should never see. Living in those conditions pushed her into wrong decisions. Eventually, she had a child she couldn't care for and gave it to a family member to raise. Depression, mental issues, rejection, abandonment and lust were the result of my mom looking for love in all the wrong places and I followed her pattern. Thus the cycle continued.

**** Whatever seed was planted in you as a child, it's important that you get to the root of it and pluck it out. Don't carry that same cycle into your family.

The ugly spirit of rejection has followed me my whole life. Feeling the need to be wanted by people, I allowed myself to get too close. I even tried to pull people along with me when God told me to try something new. There's nothing wrong with bringing people along with you on life's journeys but there has to be a balance. Sometimes God wants you to trust Him alone and take the journey by yourself. I've pulled a lot of wrong people into my circle, all for acceptance. In the process, I hurt myself along the way. To be honest, those people may have been bruised as well.

I have learned so many lessons from the mistakes and failures in my life. My past marriage and failed friendships taught me what it means to journey alone. I've learned that I'm not really alone though. I have my Abba Father with me all the way. The devil is so determined to destroy me that he tries to use those negative seeds that were planted in me as a child to destroy me. He doesn't realize, however, that they helped me become the woman of God that I am today. HA HA HA!!!!! So my declaration is that all the hell I encountered has worked out for the glory of God.

TIME TO RELEASE

Identify something's that have tried to discourage you from becoming the king or queen you are created to be? Choose today to never allow your past to label you. Pick up your pen and release.

_____

_____

_____

_____

_____

_____

_____

_____

_____

_____

_____

_____

_____

_____

_____

_____

NOTES

NOTES

CHAPTER 3
Innocence Taken Away

I WAS SEXUALLY ABUSED WHEN I was 7 years old. I was playing with my sibling and some guy a bit older than him was hanging around. I remember my brother going in the house to do something. That's when the horrible act happened. The guy told me to come to him. I went over to him and he began to pull my underwear aside and dig his hands in my vagina. "Why is he doing this to me?" kept running through my mind. I don't really remember too much of what happened after that. I believe my sibling came back and caught him. It was so long ago and nothing was done about it.

I remember after the violation, if I saw the guy in church or anywhere else, I got really nervous and scared. I would just stare into space. If you saw the movie *Home Alone*, do you remember when Macaulay Caulkin went grocery shopping and saw the two men that tried to break in his house? At that moment he dropped his groceries and was frozen with fear. That was the same feeling that plagued me with the guy who violated me. Thoughts of him touching me again haunted me, but that childhood experience awakened a sexual urge inside me that made me want those feelings over and over again.

I also remember being fondled when I was a little girl by someone on a visit from out of town. Those two experiences aroused some deep things inside me that made me really desire perverted acts at a young age. I didn't even know what sex was about but after those events took place I remember going down in this spiral of confusion. I experienced identity issues as a young girl, wondering if it was natural to be attracted to the same sex. I didn't know why, but I found myself wanting those pleasurable feelings I had felt during my molestations and attempting those acts with close female friends.

There was one situation where a friend and I were caught touching each other in a wrong way. We were told that was inappropriate and it was *not* what girls do to each other. When we got caught it was as if the darkness the enemy had been keeping me in had been exposed. For the first time I was being told what was right from wrong. From that moment I realized it was wrong so I never did it again. I thank God for us getting caught. That person saved me from going through a very perverted, destructive lifestyle.

Unfortunately, the perversion didn't stop there because in my thoughts life was full of nasty things. I looked at people in the wrong way for a long time. I remember one boy in the third grade. I wanted him to be my boyfriend and thought he liked me as well. We acted like we were going out and started holding hands in the hallway when we could. When I saw him at lunch time, I gave him notes that I had written. In middle school and high school, I became very promiscuous. Wanting to be loved, I pursued any boy I assumed liked me or who I thought was cute.

To all the young girls or teens reading this book, I just said *I* started pursuing boys. Women and girls, it is not our place to pursue the male. *It's the man's job to pursue the woman.* The Bible says in Genesis 2:18-25, *"Then the Lord God said, "It is not good for the man to be alone. I will make a helper who is just right for him. The Lord God formed from the ground all the wild animals and all the birds of the sky and* ~~He~~ *brought them to the man to see what he would call them, and the man chose a name for each one. He gave names to all the livestock, all the birds of the sky and all the wild animals, but still there was no helper just right for him. So the Lord God caused the man to fall into a deep sleep While the man slept, the Lord God took out one of the man's ribs and closed up the opening. Then the Lord God made a woman from the rib of Adam and HE BROUGHT HER TO THE MAN."*

There's a reason for those words being capitalized. They represent a major power of the role of man. Think women, we were made by God and came from man. The scripture goes on to say, *"At last!"* the man exclaimed. *"This one is bone of my bone and flesh of my flesh! She will be called woman, because she was taken from man."* This explains why a man leaves his father and mother and is joined to his wife and the two are united into one. This scripture has a symbolic purpose and I'm bringing them to your attention. See, I thought I was supposed to chase after a boy and let him know how much I cared. I felt this would cause him to want me and things would be just right, but the reality is that a female is supposed to patiently wait for Prince Charming to come to her. Proverbs 18:22 says*, "The man who finds a wife finds a treasure, and he receives favor from the Lord."* That is how God designed things to be from the beginning of time.

Fathers have A dynamic role in their little girls' lives. It is so-o-o-o-o important that they love their daughters and nurture them. They have the hearts of their daughters. That's what I missed as a little girl. Yes, I was with my grandfather until I was five and I also had my stepfather who I love to life who raised me from five years old till I felt I was grown enough to leave home. I'm thankful for those two special men who sowed priceless seeds into my life, but the reality was I was seeking my birth father! Where was he? WHY WAS HE MISSING FROM MY WORLD? I didn't do anything to make him leave. Did he even know that I existed?

I personally believe God created each birth mother and father to raise their children and love them the way He designed so they can grow up to be great people. However, this world has sin in it which makes it imperfect. Therefore, little girls and boys all over the world are being raised by only a mother or just a father. Either way, it confuses the innocent child that didn't ask to come into the world. They often grow up with abandonment issues, low self-esteem. and many more problems. That is why I went through those cycles I call 'love spells'. I was a little girl who just wanted to be loved,held, and protected by the ones that brought me into this world. That need would blow up in my face time and again.

I've always loved to cook. Growing up I watched my Mom cook and even helped occasionally, so cooking became a natural thing for me. One day while I was still in middle school, I made a treat for a boy I liked. I took the time one afternoon to make brownies. I put them in a cute wicker basket and carried them to school the next day. Well, he took my beautiful basket of brownies but paid *me* no attention! I was really hurt.

I remember another instance where I was sitting on the bus thinking about dancing for this boy who I really liked. It was Valentine's Day and I was all dressed up. In my mind some girls and I were dancing and singing *"sugar pie honey bunch, you know that I love you"*. We were singing our hearts out, but he didn't know I was alive. All this was playing in my head. I didn't realize it until later on in life that God had given me a gift for choreography and it led to many other talents that I have today.

As a young girl I loved to listen to oldies but goodies. I remember dancing in my nightgown with my neice and her friend. I gave them microphones -- actually remote controls --- and we performed my favorite song in the living room, singing AL Green's "Love and Happiness". I didn't realize it at that time but I was sowing a spirit of lust into my spirit by listening to that kind of music. I was dying to be loved and accepted for who I was, but never could find a source of real inner peace. I was looking in all the wrong places and didn't know where to find it. I was supposed to receive that from my birth mother and father but they were nowhere to be found.

TIME TO RELEASE

Have you experienced some things in your past that tried to steal your innocence away? I know what I shared with you today may have been blunt and raw. I personally believe confessions of the soul is like drain to a sink. When we release to God or someone who cares, we free ourselves from the clogged pipes in our life.

Today I want you to free yourself….

The word of God say, "So if the Son sets you free, you will be free indeed. (John 8:36) Free yourself from the pain within, after releasing. Read the poem called "FREE ME FROM MYSELF" on the next page that liberate you to another level in your life.

_____

_____

_____

_____

_____

_____

_____

_____

_____

_____

_____

_____

_____

NOTES

NOTES

_____

_____

_____

_____

_____

_____

_____

_____

_____

_____

_____

_____

_____

_____

_____

_____

_____

_____

FREE ME FROM MYSELF

Free me from the prison I'm in.
Not a physical prison with aged old bars and floors, but
The prison with old mind sets and rehearsed memories played over
And over again.
Telling me I cant do this and I will never achieve that.
This prison has held me captive to long.
Its taken over me.
Free me from this mess I'm in.
I need to be set free.
My feet are glued to the ground.
I feel like I'm in quick sand.
Im screaming from top of my voice HELP, but no one hears me.
Why? Because my cry is within .
My mouth is shut tight, but my eyes are filled with tear drops
Zillions of words are flowing from each drop.
Someone free me from this mess im in.
I'm tired of falling in the same trap.
When will I learn that everyone can't have my energy.
Everyone can't have me.
When will I learn that I can't make everyone go on the destiny that God has given to me.
No.
Everyone cant GO.
Free me God from this mess I'm in.
I'm sitting in my own filth.
I feel so weighed down .
Look at this mess I'm in.
Don't you see, How torn I am GOD?
From within.
Please come free me from myself.
Come tear down these walls
I feel like they are caving in.
Please Free me from myself .

I cant bare the pain I'm in .
They tell me, prison is worst than this, but I can't tell.
I feel like I'm in quick sand and my mind is sinking deep deep deep within.
YO…. This migraine is like aged jail cell bars that's saying "No we
can't let you go, you will stay with us until the end."
I'm screaming Free me from the chains I'm in .
God, can't you see.
This is truly not the real me.
I want to be Free
I can't take this mess anymore.
Please come set me Free.
So I can fly, like the eagle that's emerging into the sky .
So I can fly, so, so, so HIGH above all the crazy mess inside YES…
Yes the mess inside….
And then…. I heard a still soft voice reply.
My child you are FREE
I FREED you over 2,000 year ago..
But, you see..
It takes stages, Its takes you facing the old phases…
It takes receiving and then it takes you believing.
Believing, I will never leave you nor forsake you .
Believing my grace is just for you.
Believing your value comes only from me you see.
Believing, In Me and not he.
I just FREED you from yourself again, just now
Don't you know, when I speak the wind, the rain, the world has to obey my every command.
I say yes, I just FREED you just now.
So obey!

By Kawania Brickhouse

Now Check Out The Freedom Painting below. It was created just for you. My thoughts when I was painting this. I visualized myself screaming to the top of my voice the word FREEDOM……….. As I released that word it echoed across the world like a gosh of wind and waves hitting and freeing every man,woman girl or boy. That they are now FREE.

What do you see and how do the painting make you feel?

CHAPTER 4

Pornography Stage

DURING THE NEXT SEASON OF my life I started watching porn videos. I was a nosey girl and would go through my relatives' things when I was at their house. I remember going through a collection of video tapes one boring summer day. I popped one of the tapes in and there were things going on that I had never seen before. Oh my goodness!!!!!!! I was shocked and interested all at the same time. I knew it was wrong, but I continued to watch those videos whenever no one was around. I would watch those tapes and fondle myself, enjoying the stimulating feeling I experienced. I even tried to penetrate myself with objects. This went on for quite awhile.

Excuse the graphic nature of this section, but you must understand in order to be healed of the deep rooted issues in your life, you have to be willing to be transparent with yourself and others. When you're violated at any early age, it does something to you as a person. That stinking devil takes your innocence away and awakens a drive in you that can only be cured through the Blood of Jesus Christ. The heinous acts that take place in the life of a female can cripple her to the point of no return. So I say to all the young girls out there that if you have been violated, tell your parents or someone really close so you can get the help you need. ****** There are certain places that can assist you, such as the city's Social Service office, the Victim Advocate office, R AINN (Rape, Abuse and Incest National Network), and Hopeforhealing. org or Dancinginthedark.com

I recall always going to Sunday school and church as a young girl. I remember wanting to be in the Sunshine Band and be an usher at my church. In order to do anything in the church I had to be a member, so I gave my life to Christ and accepted Jesus in my heart. I believe that was a covering that helped protect me from the enemy. I was baptized and given the right hand of fellowship. I began doing activities in the church that really helped me get a better foundation with the Lord. I became really involved in the church and loved going every week. Of course that stinking Devil still bothered me in any way that he could. I was still troubled by memories of sexual abuse and perversion.

I had a counselor for years and also went to a in depth studied for a year about sexual and relational wholeness. Actually it was a class I took at about age twenty-three or twenty-four that changed my life. The group was for anyone who had dealt with brokenness or addictions. My counselor referred my former husband and myself to the group, so we attended as a couple. It was the beginning of uncovering layers of hurt in my life. The group, called Living Waters, was founded by a man from California. He is a saved man who loves the Lord but is still dealing with an attraction to the same sex.

He wanted to start sessions to help people like himself; people who loved God but couldn't understand why they still had this stronghold on their lives. When he first began the group in his home, people from his church started to come because they had these 'closet issues' and needed help. If Andrew had not stepped out on faith and started this group, those people would still be in some form of bondage today.

This ministry is structured to walk you through a healing process by going to the cross and giving God your sins. When you attend, you get corporate fellowship. A speaker reviews the lesson you had to study at home and breaks you into small groups.

Women are separated from the men and the groups have no more than five to six people with a leader who keeps everything f lowing. In these small groups you have a chance to open up and talk about the subject you have studied together. During this time, you are able to renounce the sins or hurts that were committed against you or things you may have done. The point is to discover the root issue to your brokenness. Next, you are to give it over to God so He can show you what triggers your habit or emotional problem. Once you know the source, you can cast it down and replace it with new good things.

Remember Philippians 4:8, *"whatever things are true, honest, just, pure, lovely, of good report – if there be any virtue (moral excellence) and there be any praise – think on these things"*.

This group was a good thing for my life. It allowed me to draw closer to God and open up to get help. Most of all, I realized I wasn't the only woman that had issues or a jacked up marriage. I have come to the realization that if people are willing to be transparent about their life and not walk around like they have no problems, the world would be a less bruised place. The Bible says in Ecclesiastes 4:9-11, *"Two are better than one, because they have a good return for their work: If one falls down, his friend can help him up. But pity the man who falls and has no one to help him up!"* The Bible also says in James 5:16, *"Therefore confess your sins to each other and pray for each other so that you may be healed. The prayer of a righteous man is powerful and effective."*

Now, I don't believe God puts words in His book for us to read and act on without a reason. He wants us to respond to His word and to walk it out as believers so sinners can be saved and welcomed into the family with no shame of where they've been, what they've done or what they've dealt with. It's time for people to stop condemning each other and learn to give grace and love to one another like Jesus did! Finally, I want to say that going to this group was comparable to someone having a broken leg and getting a cast put on it.

After months of the cast being on, the time comes to take it off and go to a therapist to learn how to stretch that leg out and use it again. It's a *process*; it doesn't happen overnight. You have to go through a series of sessions to function normally again. Now, in some cases, there may be a permanent scar or limp to remind you of what happened to you. The Apostle Paul, himself, was left with a thorn in his side as a reminder and we are subject to the same. This is not a bad thing because it will always remind you of God's saving power and that you didn't do it on your own. Your Father (God) walked you through the process.

***** *If you would like to find out more about this group in your local area, contact Andrew Comiskey, Desert Stream Ministries P.O. Box 17635 Anaheim Hills, CA 92687-7635, phone number 714-779-6899.*

Growing up, I spent a lot of time with my older sibling. Let me explain that the mom who raised me had three children of her own before she took in my siblings and I. They all got married, had children, and have beautiful lives. Back to my story. I was raised in the country.

Now don't get me wrong, I love the rural life now, but when I was growing up it was boring. All I could do was be a tomboy, climbing trees. In the park, I enjoyed swinging really high then jumping out of the swing. I used to kill lightning bugs and put the lights on my shirt so that when nightfall came my shirt would light up. I also killed caterpillars and frogs and caught tadpoles to put in buckets of water to keep as pets.

If I wasn't outside in the country exploring the woods, I was spending the weekend with my older sibling and her daughter. I had so much fun with them because I had a little more freedom at their home. I got so close to my third family that she became like another mother. Her daughter and I were like sisters, real tight. I love them both so much and thankful she invested in my life.

TIME TO RELEASE

Are there things that you are ashamed of? Take some time and release some things your ashamed of? I encourage you today to let it go.

Define the word shame in your own words?_____

_____

_____

Google dictionary says- a painful feeling of humiliation or distress caused by the consciousness of wrong or foolish behavior.

I personally believe shame keeps us from our purpose. When we stay caught up in our feelings. Were condemned by that little person called shame. Remember Jesus died to free you and I from the shame, pain, and guilt. Let the Lord be the lifter of your head (Psalm 3:3)

NOTES

NOTES

CHAPTER 5
Confused Years

GROWING UP WAS HARD FOR me. I was always joked on in school and on the bus by my peers. I remember being called Oprah Winfrey because I wore my hair in a mushroom cut that made me look older. I never really looked or behaved my age. I felt like an 'old spirit', as old people would say. I never really wanted to hang around kids my age. I preferred sitting around mature folk that had wisdom and listening to stories about them growing up. I remember going to across the street to a dear lady house I loved dearly and down the street to someone I called my Aunt sitting for hours just talking with them and asking a lot of questions while eating their delicious home cooked meals.

Aside from being called Oprah, I was also called Mike Tyson because I had a gap between my teeth. I used to hate it with a passion. I would cover my mouth when I talked to people at school. I got tired of being the odd ball in school, so I decided not to care or at least pretend like it. I remember saying to some of those haters, "Sticks and stones may break my bones but words will never hurt me." The truth was their words *did* hurt.

After the teasing came the bullying from a girl at my middle school. I will never forget that chick. She was another hater. She made all my friends I sat with at lunch turn against me. She spread rumors that I was talking about them, which was a lie. She just could not stand the fact that I was an outgoing girl that got along with anyone. You see, although folks joked me I was still Kawania, a girl that carried myself very well and with much maturity. Whether kids wanted to hang around me or not, I was fine. I could entertain myself. My mother put the finest clothes on me, dressing me like a little teacher every day. She kept up with the trends and I also had my sister's closet to raid. I loved that. Just about every day I had something different to wear. In retrospect, I can see why I had enemies. I was 'all that and a bag of chips.' HA HA!!!

Well, the chick that teased me used to make prank calls to my house. Even when we went on to high school the devil followed me, doing the same crap. Oh, I hated her so much! I had done nothing to her. We had a Spanish class together and she sat right behind me. Can you imagine? It was as if I was in a horror story. She was like Jason or Freddy Krueger, "I'M BACK!!!!" The words in my head were, "NO! NO! NO, go away" and one day she did. She got her butt in some deep water and was expelled from school. Hallelujah! I was so happy. She had bullied me enough.

In spite of the bullying, school was an outlet for me. I loved going because I had fun with all of my friends. I wasn't interested in the work itself unless it was art. HA! HA! I did like English to a certain degree because I was able to express myself in stories that I wrote. When we started to work on poetry, I enjoyed that as well. One of my favorite poems is by Robert Frost:

Stopping by Woods on a Snowy Evening
Whose woods these are I think I know, His house is in the village though.
He will not see me stopping here….

I have always been a creative and dramatic person. I guess that's why I took up cosmetology at Virginia Beach Technical Career School in my eleventh and twelfth grade years. I love creating new looks on people, as well as myself. Thank God for creativity. During my senior year, I was voted as Best Dressed. It was an honor to me because I love dressing for success. There are a lot of things that I could say about my years in school, but I won't. What I would really like, young girls and teenagers, to know is how important it is to love yourself and accept yourself for who you are. No matter how much people try to bully you and make fun of you, continue to be you. Tell those folk to get a life. Don't be a hater, be a participator! Life is so short.

If you walk around on eggshells trying to please others because they don't like you, then you have missed the big picture. God has uniquely designed you to be you. Embrace every piece of fabric that is yourself. There is no one like you on this earth. Maybe someone has similar characteristics, but you are unique. You were made for a purpose and plan. *"For I know the plans I have for you," says the Lord. "They are plans for good and not for disaster, to give you a future and hope (Jeremiah 29:11).* Regardless of what happened to you when you were in your childhood or adolescent years, NO bully, hater, child molester, rapist or devil in hell can stop the plans God has for you! You were made for God's greatness, so get the help you need. Whether it's talking to a pastor at your church, speaking to a therapist, or being involved in a Big Sister program, receive the help you need. Do this so you can press past the hurt and pain you have experienced, or are experiencing, to have a better future.

TIME TO RELEASE

Define the word identity in your own words ————————————

Google Definition says- the fact of being who or what a person or thing is. I say your identity comes from the Lord. I encourage you to explore what the Lord says about you in the word of God and mediate on it day and night.

Study and mediate on what the word God says about you. Below I have some scriptures I want you to look up and write them out. I personally believe when you read and then write out things to retain it better.

1 Peter 2:9_____

_____

_____

Ephesians 2:10_____

_____

_____

Corinthians 2:14-16_____

_____

_____

Galatians 2:20_____

_____

_____

NOTES

NOTES

CHAPTER 6
Living a Lie

Teenage years are hard even for the teens without issues. Parents usually say, "Oh, she's smelling herself", or at least that's a phrase I remember. The reality is, when you're a teenager you're going through mixed emotions, puberty-related changes, and peer pressure. Many girls experience being boy crazy and haters from the Himalayas during this stage. If you can relate sit back, buckle up, and let's go on a little joy ride.

In my first year of high school I knew I was "Ms. It." I always kept my hair together and stayed in the flyest clothes around. I always dressed for success and hardly ever wore sneakers. I wanted to be different. I considered myself a trend setter and I still am today. I remember the first week of ninth grade. I went to school wearing a peach and white tweed suite, some two inch heels, dangling silver and pearl chain necklace, and matching earrings. My hair was styled in a curly, bobbed, wet and wavy weave. I was the first girl at Kellam High school to rock commercial hair and look flawless.

I remember that day as if it was yesterday. I stepped in the school, not really knowing anyone, and the whispers began. I was used to it. I had been hated the year before in middle school, for no reason at all other than I simply chose to be different. Anyway, as I walked pass the lunchroom, looking for my classroom, this chick started laughing really loud. She was cracking jokes about my hair, but I didn't care. Guess what? That same chick started wearing commercial hair after she saw me with it! Not only that, she realized I really wasn't stuck up and started hanging around me. Later, during high school, she attended VoTech (the Vocational, Trade and Technical Institution) with me and became a pretty cool associate.

I said all this to say, in life young ladies, you have haters and you have participators. Remember, you're a Queen, so you never let another female make you stoop to her level. Make her come up to yours. Be loving and kind and watch God do His thing. The one who thought she hated you will realize how silly she's acting and will check herself. In Matthew 7:12, the word of God says, *"Do unto others as you would have them do unto you"*. I do my very best to treat people the way I want to be treated and I pray those who are reading this book do the same. Everybody desires to be loved and accepted whether they say it or not.

My lying years were filled with many shades of colors. What I mean by that is, there was always something new going on in my little life at that time. I remember begging my mother every weekend to let me spend the night over my girlfriends' homes so that we could go hang out at the mall or go to a party or just do something. As I told you before, growing up in the country was boring. Nothing to do but eat, sleep, listen to the birds chirp or frogs make their mating noise. I did go to church on Sundays, which I enjoyed. I had a particular set of friends that I would hang with and we would get into things we had no business doing.

One of my friends, who I will call Mary, and I sneaked out of her parents' home early one morning around twelve o' clock to go to this party that we weren't suppose to attend. Well, we put on our grown up wardrobe and headed down the street in the pitch dark. A police car pulled up beside us as we strolled down the street thinking we were grown.

The cop asked where we were going and how old we were. Well, we were caught red handed, big time. The police made us get in his car and took us back to Mary's house. When her parents came to the door it was over for us. I remember begging Mary's mom not to tell my parents because I knew I wouldn't live to see the next year. Thank God she didn't tell. Now that I think back to that moment, I see how stupid I was to be strolling down the street that late. What if someone had kidnapped us, raped us, and left us for dead? I wouldn't be writing this book today.

As a teenager you just think about having fun and living for the moment. The reality is that you have to walk in wisdom and obedience to live a long good life. The scripture says, *"Honor your Mother and Father and your days shall be long"*(Exodus 20:2). So many teens nowadays don't live past 13 or 16 years of age because of the big word – SIN!!

With the same group of friends I had back then, I experienced more things than my hands can type. There's one particular event I will never forget; the day I lost my virginity. It wasn't a planned event and if I could change the hands of time I would redo some things. I was hanging with my friend Mary again. She knew this guy in he neighborhood who knew my older brother. One day we went over to his house. My friend was in one room and I went to another room with the guy. He and I were playing around, wrestling, and one thing led to another. How stupid could I have been?

I didn't really know the guy other than he was a friend of my brother's and went to our high school. He and I had no relationship, but I allowed him to kiss and touch me. In less than a few minutes, I lost my prize possession to him. I remember it being painful, but since we were trying to be quiet in the room, I muffled my cry. Because of curiosity, this sneaky act stole my purity. Now that I look back at the moment, I cringe. I gave away something so precious to someone I didn't even care about! He was just someone popular at my school. I would never have any form of commitment from him. I was just a score on his football field of conquests. That door of promiscuity opened up many other sexual moments as my high school years slowly dissolved before my eyes.

To all my teenagers reading this book, if you're a virgin, *please stay that way!* God has designed you to give your sexual purity to the partner you marry for life. Don't share your gift with anyone who doesn't value you. If you don't value yourself, I encourage you to get to know the real you and learn to cherish your body. God said your body is the temple of the Holy Spirit and you should be a good steward over it. That means honor it and treat it with respect. Don't cast your pearls upon 'swine'. Pearls are jewels that are kept in a jewelry box for special protection. When they are worn, they are guarded and treasured by one who knows and appreciates their worth.

God has intended for all of us to enjoy real love one day, but He wants us to experience it with Him first, so He can mold us to properly to understand the depth of love. Song of Solomon 2:15 says*, "How beautiful you are, my darling! Oh, how beautiful ! Your eyes are doves."* Doves have perennial vision and only can see what is right in front of them. They can't see anything else except what they are gazing on at that moment. That's the type of vision God desires for you to have for Him. Put your attention and focus totally on His Glory.

When God sends a prospect into your life that may one day become your significant other, you should have that same focus on them. In the above scripture text, the Lover was talking to his beloved. He was expressing his heart to her letting her know how beautiful she was as she stared into his eyes. She had dove's eyes. To all my teens out there, you will meet someone of the opposite sex that you are attracted to -- a dime a dozen. Don't lose your focus on what matters most; live life with no regrets. Put your gaze on Christ first and your dreams second. At the right time, God will allow those dreams to become a reality.

Life has many lessons for you to learn. Take each test for what it is, but don't make dumb mistakes like I did. I was so caught up in having a "boyfriend" that I couldn't see clear. I should have been more concerned about my grades in school. I wasn't a bad student, but my education wasn't my major focus. I did what was necessary to pass classes, but I didn't put my all in school. I didn't even get involved in sports or try out for different clubs in school like I should have. I had a voice back then. What a difference I could have made! I was a great encourager; a talented young lady that had values. I could have been class president in school. Well, the past is the past so I won't harp on what I 'could of, should of, or would have done'. I'm just making point that you matter. It's so important that you put your all into who God created you to be.

There's only one you, so make a difference in the world. Explore your gifts and talents and allow them to come alive while you're young and vibrant. Let it work for your good. Don't waste precious moments getting high off of weed or getting laid by the popular guy in school. In the end you will regret it.

TIME TO RELEASE

Do you have any regrets? _____

_____

_____

_____

_____

_____

_____

_____

_____

_____

_____

_____

_____

_____

Someone once told me, live life with no regrets. We all think about the what would have; the should haves or what we could have done different. The reality is, whatever we have experienced has made us into who we are crated to be. So embrace them all.

NOTES

NOTES

CHAPTER 7

False Freedom

I LEFT MY HOMETOWN WHEN I was twenty years old. I was so excited about getting my first apartment. My true freedom was beginning; at least that's what I thought. I was fed up with the rules at my family's home and I wanted to go and come as I pleased. I did not want any more curfews. I was grown.

I remember taking my Mom and Dad out to lunch to break the news that I was leaving home. They didn't say much. Hey, what could they say? I was making my own money and would be paying for everything myself. I had a great job working at *Empowered Images* as a cosmetologist. I had a great boss who pulled the best out of me and challenged me to never settle for less.

After moving into my apartment, I quickly turned it into my quiet oasis. I loved it! I would sit back on my couch after a hard day of work, drink juice from my pretty glassware and turn on some relaxing soft music to vibe with. I was enjoying the good life. At that time I wasn't involved in any serious relationship. Actually I felt a relationship would be more of a problem. I needed that time to myself, to get to know me, Kawania. I needed to embrace who I truly was and accomplish all the great goals I had set for myself.

I was a busy bee back then. I had an older cousin who I tagged along with because she worked in the medical field and I liked to shadow her at work. I remember being involved with nursing homes. I would go and visit the elderly. I would help however I could or just go around speaking with patients. I even volunteered my time to do their hair, occasionally. I enjoyed spending time with the sweet, mature people God placed in my life.

Life was getting better each and every day. My cousin, two of my coworkers, and I started a group called Virtuous Women. We spent a lot of time volunteering at a recreational center helping the youth with their education. Man, now that I think back on those days, I had no worries. I was stress free, but I complained all the time because I had no man and all my friends did. I remember one particular day I went to the barber shop to get my hair cut and my eyebrows done before heading to school. I had a particular barber I saw who was like a big brother and father figure to me. He always listened to me vent about all my male woes and about there being no good men in the world.

One day he called me at work to ask me if it was alright to give my number to a young fellow he thought would be great for me. I asked him if the man was saved because I didn't want to deal with any more drama. He said the guy was and I would be pleased. Now, before I go any further, I would like to say that prior to meeting this young man all my other relationships had ended due to them cheating or relocating. I had had no good relationship experiences over the years and I was so young. I really wasn't as ready for a relationship as I thought.

The young man's name was 'Billy'– at least that's what I'll call him. He called me and we chatted over the phone for the next couple of days and decided to meet that coming weekend at the Fest going on in downtown Norfolk. I met him and we had a great time at dinner. Afterward, we sat in the car for an hour or so talking about life. We learned some interesting things about each other. One great thing that we had in common was being in the cosmetology business; he was a barber. We both also came from broken families. Neither of us had been raised fully by our birth parents so that meshed us even closer together. We understood each other.

Weeks went by and I grew fonder of him every day. He treated me like a queen, taking me to the finest restaurants, to production plays, and buying me beautiful gifts all the time. We stayed on the phone for hours talking and reading the Word together. That really drew me to him even more. I loved the fact that he knew the Word of God. I was attracted to the God in him. He also helped me with issues that I had to deal with concerning family. I had never met a man of God that understood me. I was amazed. At that time in my life I was hungry for God and His word. I wanted to know all that I could know about God on a higher level. I wanted God to be more than just a distant lord sitting on the throne. I wanted to know Him as my friend and Father. Being with this young fellow gave me a sense of closeness to God. That was it!!!!

Then the worse thing happened to jack up the relationship. We had sex.

Why did I mix the friendship with sexual relations? I don't know!!!!! Yes, I do know. It was because I wanted this man to know me at a deeper level and I wanted to feel loved. Yes, it was wrong and I asked God to forgive me, but it became an addiction that I could not stop. For the first time in my life, I actually **_enjoyed_** having sex! I had had sex with past boyfriends, but it was different with Billy. Maybe it was because he was more experienced.. I'm not sure, but we couldn't keep our hands off of each other. After awhile I started to experience guilt, shame, and remorse whenever we had sex.

Other than this blot, it seemed as though we had a great relationship. I had met his family and he had met mine. However, something just wasn't sitting right with me. I could feel that Billy was hiding something from me. Whenever we spent time together his darn phone or pager was always going off and that bothered the mess out of me. On top of that, he never introduced me to any of the friends he hung with when I wasn't around. I started wondering if he had told them about me. I remember expressing my feelings about it and the discussion resulted in us breaking it off. Talk about extreme! I realized I wanted more than what I was getting. I wanted a commitment but he had insisted on just being friends (with benefits), so we went our separate ways.

I was sad because I had developed a bond with this man and spiritually I had soul ties with him because of the sexual relations. On the f lip side, I had a sense of relief because I wasn't sinning anymore. That had bothered me big time! I hated disappointing God and having to show up in His face constantly with the same sin, asking him to forgive poor Kawania once again. The truth was we had been living a double life. Behind closed doors we did 'the do' but in front of our family, friends and the church we acted as if we were true saints. Now the secret life of sexual sin that I had been living had come to an end. At least that's what I thought.

In the month of January, less than a month after breaking up with Billy, I discovered I was PREGNANT. What was I to do? I prayed for my cycle to come on, but it never showed up. I took test after test and the results were the same each time, _pregnant_. I decided to tell Billy. I remember him picking me up and going to this place so Icould get another test result. We looked at other 'options', but I was too scared to do anything so we left. We told his family that I was pregnant and they took it pretty well. His Aunt a sweet woman, became a wonderful source of support in my life from that point on. Then came the big event that I feared the most, telling _my_ Mom and Dad.

I recall the day we drove to their house. It seemed like the longest drive ever. When we broke the news to my folks I released a sigh of relief, but they were not happy at all. They wanted to know what Billy's plans were. He told them he was going to take care of the child but that he was not ready to get married. They were less than pleased about that. My Mom and Dad always wanted the best for me and I know it crushed their hearts to find out that their unmarried child was having a baby. I was so young and I had just left home less than a year ago. After I left my family's home that day, I didn't see them again until it was time for me to give birth to my daughter.

August 19, 2000 was a very special day. My baby girl came into the world. Everybody, it seemed, was at the hospital. His Aunt was there the whole time and video taped it all. She was so beautiful and I adored my little angel. Right after I gave birth, Billy blessed me with a couple of gifts. One of them was a white f luffy teddy bear that had a box attached to it. Inside was a ring. Billy proposed right in the room and I said yes. I was full of joy that he wanted to be with me, but to be honest with you, I really wasn't ready for marriage. In retrospect, it may not have been a good thing because two broken people can't do much for each other, except make a broken mess.

Everything in my life at the time was exciting and new but seemed to be happening so fast. I was living on my own in a nice apartment then boom, here comes my first child and boom again, I was planning my big wedding. I had a lot of emotions going on. We had been hypocrites and now we wanted to cover it up by trying to fix the issue. In reality, the true problem wasn't being fixed at all. We were making things worse. I was getting ready to jump the broom in six months. I would be with this man for the rest of my life! Actually I wanted it but was I really ready for such a major commitment? We were both so young. I was only twenty- one and he was just twenty-six.

We came from two totally different worlds. I was a sheltered girl who grew up in the country for the majority of my life and was still festering with wounds of rejection and abandonment in the fiber of my core. I was a very naive gal that had been looking for love in all the wrong places. Billy was raised in city and went through difficult things in his past that had planted seeds of rejection in his life. He had turned to the streets, selling drugs and getting involved in things that put him in jail during his teens. He wasn't released until he was an adult so his youthful years were forfeited. When Billy got out, he had gone to college and started rebuilding the life he had lost. I believe when we met each other we were at places in our lives where we had established ourselves and were beginning to enjoy our singleness.

Sadly, when people are incomplete they settle for less in order to feel whole. They link up with someone else sharing a like spirit. This is what took place with Billy and me. Ecclesiastes 3:1 says, *"There is a time for everything and a season for every activity under heaven."* It was NOT our time to get married. So what if we had a child? Just 34 because you have someone's baby doesn't mean you have to marry them, especially, when you're outside the will of God. Warning signs were blazing, but we ignored them. We decided to come together in a union that was doomed to fail, caught up in planning a two hundred and fifty guest wedding.

Ecclesiastes 8:1 says, *"Who is like the wise man? Who knows the explanation of things? Wisdom brightens a man's face and changes it's hard appearance."* We should have sought wisdom from the Lord and waited so we would know the best course to take for our lives. I admit we had grown fonder of each other while I was pregnant and he went to every doctor's appointment I had. He did anything for me but something just wasn't right. I still didn't trust him and God had visited me in many dreams showing me the truth about the man I felt I was in love with. He really didn't belong to me. There had been other women in the beginning while he and I were dating. He tried to keep it from me but I found out. That was one of my reasons for leaving him before I found out I was having his child.

The wise thing he and I should have done during that time of our lives, instead of getting married, was to concentrate on raising our child. He should have continued on with his life and I needed to have done the same. He and I believed in God but we didn't truly *trust* God and that's where true wisdom lies. We were members of an awesome church that tried to lead us down the path of rebuilding our lives together and becoming one. We went through the required premarital counseling but that wasn't enough. We still needed time for healing. Only time and God could heal the wounds both of us had experienced over the years or reverse the effects of the foul seeds we planted by having sex out of wedlock.

We were married on a cold winter day and my beautiful daughter, was dressed just like her mommy. We wore cream satin dresses that had beautiful rhinestones embroidered in them. It was a beautiful occasion and the wedding was the talk of the town. Pause... I'm struggling to type how I truly feel about that day. I really don't care to go back in time and bring up any of those old memories, but it's important for me to give you some details that will help you not make the same mistakes in your life. Lord help me.

I remember waking up that morning and opening my Bible to the book of Genesis. I read how God put Adam to sleep in order to form Eve. What really stuck out to me in those verses is in Genesis 2:23-24, *"The man said, this is now bone of my bones and flesh of my flesh: she shall be called Woman for she was taken out of man. For this reason a man will leave his father and mother and be united to his wife, and they will become one flesh. The man and his wife were both naked, and they felt no shame."* After reading those verses that morning, I felt as if my marriage was being blessed by God because of the word that I had read. We would be one after the wedding ceremony. That's what I wanted. That was always my desire, to be loved and to love my mate with all my heart. It seemed all too good to be true. The scripture says in Mark 10:9, *"What God has joined together let no man tear asunder."* The real question I had struggled with was, "Had God joined us together or was this our doing? I think that's a very important question every couple needs to ask themselves because a lot of couples come together outside the will of God.

Now that I think about it, I've learned that every man who pursues you is not meant for you to acknowledge. Billy and I fornicated repeatedly, causing anything we could have had to be jacked up from that point. In addition, I had enough signs from God concerning Billy's involvement with other women and the dumb lies he told me. Even his own family members told me to leave him alone, but NO, I chose to try to fix the man. Now how many women have been there and done that? The truth is you can't fix nobody, not even your darn self. You need God to fix you-- if you truly want it done the right way. You have to allow the Holy Spirit to come inside of you and renew the right spirit in you. Oh why, why, why, did I get married?

CLUE 1: WHY I WASN'T SUPPOSED TO GET MARRIED !

What I remember most about that day was my face being hard and tight. Now I know that sounds a little crazy, but I had a friend do my hair and makeup. I loved my hair but my face felt tight and I could hardly smile. The problem was she had put some all day cream on my face so I wouldn't mess up my makeup, but I didn't need that. I was a young chicken at the time. My skin was just fine without all of that extra stuff. Well, after my face was finished I got dressed. Who should come in the room at that moment with her big mouth asking me what was wrong with my face? My lovely sibling. It never fails for her to be real and give you her honest opinion about any situation. Well, she did! I was nervous already because I was about to walk down the aisle. My other siblings eventually kicked her out of the room.

One major thing in every wedding for a woman is making sure she has the best wedding pictures EVER!!!!!!!!!!! I mean EVER! Well, I was disappointed. My pictures sucked!!! I mean SUCKED and it wasn't because of the photographer. It was because my makeup was jacked up. My face was the lightest thing on my body. What in the ham sandwich? I remember when my picture book came back after the wedding I was mad as I don't know what; but what could I have done then? The wedding was long gone. I wanted to blame Billy because he hadn't let me get my makeup done by s a profound makeup artist named Patrick Bradley. Billy was jealous and didn't want no other man working on his soon- to- be wife. LOL. Man, it's funny but that's the truth. I saw that as the first sign of my marriage not being meant to be.

My pictures were horrible! Yes, I was still beautiful regardless of the makeup. In my opinion, if the marriage was truly meant to be, my makeup would have been fierce because I'm a Queen who is fierce all the time. Can you relate? It felt like an omen. I mean God created Kawania to beautify people, places and things. That's why I'm a cosmetologist, makeup artist, painter and interior designer. I represent Beauty. So why should my wedding memories include disgusting pictures like that? Ok, people, please don't think I'm stuck up. I'm not. It's confidence. Something I lacked too many years and now I have it, so I walk in it because my Abba Father orders me to.

Billy was not the man God wanted me to be with and one day I will get a chance to do it the right way. My pictures will be f lawless this time, BABY, because I will do my own face. I will represent myself— Global Royalty, a well known franchise. A palace created for Queens and Kings to be pampered, beautified and much more.

CLUE 2 : WHY I WASN'T SUPPOSED TO GET MARRIED.

I would like to warn you that it's so important to abstain from sex until you're married because I believe it takes the fun out of things if you have sex before you tie the knot. A pastor I know says, "The beauty of marriage is in the exploration". Exploring your significant other too soon will destroy the true intimacy you can experience by waiting for that lovely wedding night. Your new mate should be like a puzzle that only you can solve through doing intimate, loving, desirable things that rock their world. God designed sex for marriage. I will admit the sex was awesome when we were sinning. At least I thought it was, but I believe the devil gives you that illusion to keep you going back for more and more. Therefore, you never stop fornicating. The truth is, when you get down before marriage you open yourself up for disappointment because on your wedding night there's nothing new. If you two have already smacked it up, f lipped and rubbed it down what else is there to explore on your wedding night? Not a darn thing! Can I get an amen? Yeah, you can now finally have sex with God's approval and that's great, but you already had a taste test!

CLUE 3 : I WASN'T SUPPOSED TO GET MARRIED.

We went to the Bahamas for our honeymoon. We were both excited. It was somewhere we had never been. Here's the kicker, we almost overslept that morning and almost missed our f light to Florida. When we arrived in Florida we boarded the cruise ship and settled in. A day later I was starting to feel some nausea. I assumed it was from the boat. Of course that wasn't the case! I was pregnant but at that time I didn't know it. When we returned back home I made the discovery. This would be child number two.

Wow, what in the ham sandwich! I had just married Billy not too long after having my first child seven months ago and now I was knocked up again. I was Fertile Myrtle!

Ok, back to my story. When we arrived at our first island, we got off the ship and started exploring. Busy Bees, we couldn't stay in one place and chill. I don't remember which island, it could have been Freeport but I'm not sure. We took a cab to venture further into town and went to the different vendors. Finally, we settled down on the beautiful beach. The water was so clear it was breath taking. Mr. Billy wanted to go jet skiing. I had never been before, nor had he.

On one of the Island, some men took us to a boat so we could start our adventure. The man looked at me and asked if I was getting on with Billy and I said yes. I guess he thought I was crazy because Billy did not know how to work the thing and there I was jumping on the back of the skis like he was experienced! Off we went in the water. Billy started off slow and then he sped up more and more until I was screaming for my life as I realized how far we were from the shore. I begged him to take me back to the shore, which he did then took off again.

Once on land, I chilled on the beach relaxing in the sun. Billy eventually finished skiing and joined me. We decided to shop but never paid attention to the time. When we realized what time it was, we decided to get back to the ship because it would soon set sail for the next island. We caught a cab and the driver drove as fast as he could to the ship but guess what, we missed it. I know, RIGHT! What in the ham sandwich! We were stuck on that island for the night. We had very little money with us because all of our belongings were on the ship. We walked around that evening looking like two goof balls. This was our honeymoon and we were stranded on an island.

We slept in some hotel that was not up to the standards we were used to, but it was just for the night. Well, silly me was scared. I get so spooky at times. I refused to cut the lights off because I saw a roach. OMG I hate those suckers. The next morning we rushed to the only little airport they had on that island to catch a f light to the next island. It was somewhat of a wait. We finally boarded a small plane to the next island. When we saw our cruise ship I was so relieved.

Looking back over those years, this event was another clue for me that I was not supposed to have married Billy at that time. Oh God, thank you for grace and mercy! Let me be real with you. I don't regret all I experienced in that marriage. It made me a better woman. If I had not experienced the tests I went through, I wouldn't be the woman I am today or know God at the level I do. Remember the scripture, *"All things work together for the good of those who are called to his purpose,"* (Romans 8:28). Just think if I hadn't gone through that crap in my marriage or all the other things in my younger years, I wouldn't have this book for you to read nor my testimony. The bible says in Revelation 12: 11, *"And they conquered him by means of the blood of the Lamb and by the utterance of their testimony."*

My life is not my own. I belong to God. I have to share what I walked through so I can help the next person overcome her obstacles. We are all covered by the blood of the Lamb. What would we do if we didn't have the blood of Christ to cleanse us of our sins? Everything I experienced is under the blood. Thank God for that! The scripture goes further by telling us to share our testimony. It's not easy to share your personal shortcomings or experiences, but we need not love our lives more than witnessing to the lost. It's all for the glory of the Lord. After returning home I went to the doctor because I knew I was having another little one. My life was going to be different for sure now. My one bedroom apartment was alright for the three of us, but after learning of my pregnancy. Billy wanted to purchase our first home so we could have more room. We had a lot on our plates. A new marriage, one baby and another on the way.

God provided tremendously for us. Before little Jr. was born we found a home but didn't move in until after he came. Life seemed pretty good for us. I saw little signs indicating problems were brewing, but I choose to ignore them. Billy started coming home late some nights from work. That bothered me but he reassured me it was all business. I knew the truth. Like I told you before; I knew from the get go we shouldn't have gotten married so soon but f lesh wants what it wants. I was beginning to pay the consequences for my actions.

Pause for a moment!!!! I would like to say to my readers that when you see signs, don't just push them away like they don't exist; deal with them head on. If you don't, it will bite you in the butt later like mine did.

Billy's behavior became a pattern, but I felt I should take matters into my own hands. Oh why, oh why? He hid his activities of pleasure behind work. Instead of coming home in the evening to spend time with his family; he stayed out late, and oh how I hated that! He and I had many knock down drag out fights. I acted as though I could beat his tail; but I knew I couldn't. I would get in his face accusing him of things, and yes, I even put my hands on him. I would throw objects and call him every name in the book. I was mad.

I just wanted him to commit to our family instead of hanging out in the streets all different times of the night. Was I not good enough? Did I not do enough? What did he want from me? I worked hard just like he did. Raising two little ones wasn't an easy job. Keeping a home together, cooking dinner, and cleaning was my job and I took it seriously. I wanted to know why he didn't want to be home with us at night and I eventually found out the truth after I began snooping around for information. I found women's business cards and phone numbers. I questioned him and even called some of the women myself. Some told me the truth and others played the game. The bottom line was my main source of pain was living in the same house with me. Every day he would lie down with me like life was good, knowing he was living another life that no one knew about except him and God.

I tried so many different things to keep his attention. We went out on dates and I would do different things for special occasions to show him how much I cared. I was his freak in the bed. Our children are proof. I wasn't a boring woman. What he wanted I gave to him. The division that took place right before my very eyes was a hard pill to swallow. I didn't know what to do other than run to God with all my prayers and petitions. I sought counseling to release the pain I was experiencing.

I remember waking up one night at two in the morning and rolling over to my spouse to get some. You see we had a routine of really getting our groove on in the wee hours of the morning. It was a normal routine and it was usually the best time because we had young ones and we wanted to make sure they were sound asleep. Well, this particular morning I was longing for some TLC and we went at it; but for some reason he wasn't into it like I wanted him to be, which bothered me. He gave me what I wanted but it wasn't like the usual. It was rough and hard and I felt like an object being used. I felt dirty. The way he handled my precious body wasn't right at that moment. After we finished, he laid back down and I went downstairs to lay on the couch and cry my heart out to God.

At that very moment, God began to speak to me about what happened earlier when I woke up to be intimate with my spouse. *God* wanted to talk to me. *He* wanted intimacy from his daughter. I learned in those wee morning hours that God was longing for a deeper walk with me. Every time I woke up early did not mean that I was to turn over for my husband to stroke my flesh. There were destiny appointments, or dates, that God had set aside for Him and me so I could reach another level in my spiritual walk.

Over the next few years, things began to change for me. I really began to draw closer to God and chose to ignore a lot of stuff that I saw my husband doing that I knew was dead wrong. I would run to my Father with all my issues and I even began a women's prayer group that became a great success. Things were changing for the better in my spiritual life, but in the natural my husband was growing further away from me. We opened up our first beauty and barbershop together, which took a lot of time and energy from the both of us for it to be successful. Not too long after opening the business I discovered once again that I was pregnant. I believe this added extra pressure for both of us in our already strained marriage, but the new little one was not to blame -- he was a blessing from God.

TIME TO RELEASE

Do you remember a time in your life, that you thought you was free, but you actually wasn't? Write that experience down. What did you learn from that season?

_____

_____

_____

_____

_____

_____

After reading through this chapter. Have you ever had signs that you wasn't suppose to do something, but you chose to ignore it anyway? What was the outcome of ignoring the signs? Are you experiencing any effects in your life today? What valuable lesson did you learn from that lesson?

_____

_____

_____

_____

_____

_____

NOTES

NOTES

CHAPTER 8

The Break Down

THE HOLIDAYS WERE APPROACHING AND I had this gut feeling about issues that I had chosen to ignore for a very long time. I had enough of keeping my mouth closed. I decided to go off and when I did…I really went off. I wanted to know the truth about everything. I did not want any more lies told or gifts given to keep my mouth closed. My husband was mine but why didn't I feel like it? I had to get to the bottom of it.

One evening, before we headed out of town to see my folks in Philly for Thanksgiving, I decided to ask Billy who he was involved with and I wasn't taking "nobody" for an answer. He broke down and told me that the women I accused him of seeing were not fictitious. This had been going on for about four years; there had been some one night stands. I was heartbroken and had a mouth full of every M.F. I could say.

I didn't know what to do. Yeah, I know I should have packed my bags to leave; but I was pregnant again and I truly didn't want to tear our family apart. I made him promise me that when we returned from Philly we would start counseling together at the church. He agreed and that's how it went down.

Counseling seemed to help for a period of time. The test was always what happened when we left the office and had to actually put what we learned to work. Weeks went by and Billy did pretty well with accountability. Things seemed better, but were they really? I remember going in the hospital for a planned cesarean to deliver my son. A few days later my girlfriend and her husband brought me home from the hospital because

Billy was on the grind either at the salon or his other job as a social worker. I hated that when I needed him most he seemed consumed with work. I sucked it up though and dealt with it. I was happy to have others who cared enough to be present for me.

I had planned to have my tubes tied, but I was too chicken to go through with it. So instead I had the Mirena inserted after my six weeks checkup. It proved to be the best birth control for me. It was the key to keeping Fertile Myrtle from getting pregnant. At that point in my life I sure didn't need any more children. My hands were already full as a mother and a wife. Besides that I was busy playing detective and trying to keep control of our relationship.

I truly enjoyed being a mother. It was a natural thing for me. My babies were my world. I wanted the best for them and their future. I would go through hell and high water to protect them. That was one of my reasons for never leaving the marriage. I didn't want to fail them and I didn't want them to grow up without their real father in their life. I wanted them to have a better life than Billy and I had growing up. I know now as I reflect on the situation that I actually put my children in a bad environment.

I know that no family is perfect and everybody goes through things, but children are not meant to endure living in abusive environments. The environment that we had created for our children was not a good one. They saw mommy and daddy fighting all the time. Yes, I admit I was a fighter. I said some foul cuss words out of my mouth to verbalize how I felt about the things he was doing to me. Over the years I experienced two black eyes on two separate occasions. I know Billy had no business hitting me, but I had no business attacking him either.

Ladies, word to the wise, keep your hands to yourself. It's not worth it. You can't beat the man in most cases. Just get up and walk away. Stay away from the knives too because they ain't worth it either. You probably will do something that you will regret for the rest of your life.

Billy and I were a little ruthless when it came to our anger. Thank God we didn't kill each other. I remember when I went to jail once because I pushed him in front of the police. They handcuffed me and took me away when *he* was the one that was supposed to go because he had just choked the crap out of me. That was a day to remember. I sat in that jail thinking I was about to rot to death, but I "knowed there was a GOD!!" (from *The Color Purple*). LOL!!! I remember crying my little eyeballs out. I wasn't a criminal! I felt my actions were justified because that crazy man had a Sex Demon in Him. I was determined to tame it with either my anointing oil or my fist. LOL… Look where I ended up.

After they kept me in the cell for about two hours they took my fingerprints and released me. My girlfriend came to pick me up. I was so humiliated. I prayed no one would ever find out about that story but somehow my nosey older sister found out. One of her friends forged her name on a check of hers and because our names are similar to mine. They assumed it was me. Anyway, she told the officer at the police station her sister would never do such a thing and they showed her a picture of me in the computer from when I was booked for that drama with Mr. Man. I didn't want to get into details with my sister about my personal life. I told her to mind her business. That drove a bigger gap between us; but I didn't want to involve my family in my issues. I felt like I could work them out on my own. Maybe if I had opened up, I would have received help and gone on with life sooner.

Pursuant to that major life changing experience, Billy and I had to go to court. Per the judge's order, I had to take anger management classes. That was an enlightening experience. I went to a group setting on a weekly basis for two months. We all had to introduce ourselves, give our reasons for attending the group, and work on exercises to help us with our anger. I thought to myself when I went to meetings, "Why in the world am I here?" I felt like I had nothing in common with those women. All I had done was push my husband in front of the police and they sent me to jail. *I* was the one with the scars on my neck that he had put there.

The truth was, I did have a lot of anger hemmed up inside of me. There was something going on in the spiritual realm with my Father and me. God wanted me to address *me*. He wanted me to take a good look at myself and figure out why I was doing the things I was doing. I had been trying to get back at Billy for the sins he was committing against me, but Romans 12:19 expresses the Lord's command that "Vengeance is mine." It never said vengeance was Kawania's.

The reality was that I was committing a sin as well. When I found out that Billy had cheated on or lied to me, I sinned by taking matters into my own hands. I fought back with my fist and the objects that I threw at him. Even the words I used to tear down his spirit were sinful. No person deserves to be called a hoe and the other words I said that I refuse to print in this book. I'm sure you have an idea.

The Bible says in Galatians 6:8-10, *"For he that soweth to his flesh shall of the flesh reap corruption; but he that soweth to the Spirit shall of the Spirit reap life everlasting. Let us not be weary in well doing: for in due season we shall reap, if we faint not. As we have therefore opportunity, let us do good unto all men, especially unto them who are of the household of faith."* I believe these scriptures are self explanatory but I would like to add a small note. No matter how a person treats you, it is better to love on them a little harder than to stab them in the back like they have done you. What will you really profit in that revenge? Isaiah 50:4-9 says, *"God is the vindicator."*

I have learned through my many trials that He can deal with a person better than any of us can. It's amazing what simple things you can learn when God makes you sit down or puts you under arrest to get your attention. That year I began to embrace God in a whole new way. I was learning what true love and sacrifice were all about. All the lessons took place through the episodes from hell that occurred in my own home. The average person that experiences offenses usually runs because they don't feel up to the task. While I didn't feel excited about being abused and used, I'm not a quitter. In the midst of the storm, I decided to run to God for my comfort. He allowed me to cry my heart out to Him. I knew that He was the only one that truly understood.

I sought additional counseling for Billy and me. We also got involved with some deeper help from a local church that lasted for a very long time. I realized I had to take a good look at myself. God was purging some deep rooted issues out of me and He was using my spouse to do it. I know you are about say, "But Kawania, you didn't deserve any of that drama that was going on in your life." That's true. None of us deserve certain things and, yes, you are supposed to love yourself by not settling for less. Besides all of that, God opened my eyes and began to show me things. MYSELF, for one!

I started to see a sickness in myself that truly needed help. I was a young woman who ran to a man for comfort and put him on a pedestal where he didn't belong. Billy could never fill the inner void that I was experiencing. Yes, we were married and there were certain things that he was obligated to do... like be a faithful husband and friend. Yet, I should have never put certain expectations on him because he is a creation, human, just like I am. I needed to *'look toward the hills from which my help came'* (Psalms 121:1).

As time progressed I began to cope better with my life and created a routine with my children that truly helped me focus more. I became the best darn mother I could be, spending quality time with them at home when I wasn't at work. I cooked marvelous meals for them and turned our house into a home with the blessed hands God had given me. Not only was I a hairstylist and makeup artist, I was also a designer that loved to decorate and change trash into treasure. I only wish I could have made that transformation with my marriage. I took old pieces of furniture and restained or refurbished them. I painted the walls bright, inviting colors to bring our home to life and really just did anything to beautify it. As I allowed the Lord to work on me and stopped focusing my attention on all the negativity between Billy and myself, I began to realize the many gifts God had placed inside of me.

I was truly amazed what the Lord did through my hands. I had a friend at my church that showed me how to sew and use my sewing machine. I went to work making window curtains, shower curtains and even small outfits for my daughter. My life was taking a turn for the better again. I was a little busy bee at home. I had become a Martha Stewart. I also had a strict schedule with my babies in the evening time. After picking up my little daughter from her Christian Academy (all of my children started school at the age of three), we would go home and initiate our routine of homework, dinner, baths, Bible reading, and prayer before bedtime. They would all be sleep by seven thirty or eight o'clock in the evening. I did not play. When you have three children, you have to have a schedule if you want to truly have peace of mind and some kind of time for yourself. It is very important.

After they went to bed I would light some candles and turn some soft music on to relax or just read the Bible or self help books. At that point in my life I was looking for anything to show me how to work on being the best me. Billy had given me a book written by Joyce Meyers entitled *Learn How to be Yourself.* That book really blessed my life. I dissected it and blessed other people I knew with what I learned from it. I also joined a women's group and studied the lessons called *Out of Egyp*t which taught us to eat only when we were hungry. I actually lost thirty pounds by the end of the course. I was truly amazed. God was doing a total makeover on me.

Then I placed my heart into going back to school because I left at twenty when I got pregnant with daughter. I decide to take Psychology. It was something I wanted to do back in high school and I knew it would go well with my ministry work because I loved the word of God and I wanted to help people. I was accepted and truly enjoyed it. I was blessed with some scholarships and grants, which gave me the luxury of not paying a dime. I learned so much there and met so many new friends. I knew school was for me, but then something happened. I gave it up. "Why", you ask? Certain classes had become somewhat overwhelming at times. I remember talking to Billy about it. "Kawania, school isn't for everybody! If it's too much, then let it go." So that's what I did. I wish now that he had pushed me to stay in because it really would have blessed my life.

I did other things to keep myself preoccupied, like working for Mary Kay. I was an excellent sales rep. I sold a lot of products and even started building a team. I went to several conferences and all the meetings. I was hyped. I had a great strategy for getting ahead. Being a hairstylist and makeup artist, in conjunction with Billy and me owning the salon, I decided to merge my talents. I started having parties at the salon. I got different clients to host parties and I taught them how to cleanse their skin and apply their makeup. In return they purchased all of their products from me. I served hors d'oeuvres and played music as some of the women did a little modeling. By that time they were feeling real good. At the end of those parties I was pocketing good money, if you know what I mean. It was great.

Well, that venture only lasted for a short season because I was introduced to another makeup line that I currently use called *Sasha Cosmetics*. I was turned on to this line because the makeup is truly f lawless and it catered to my skin completion. The line was created in Trinidad for women with yellow skin tones. I took some samples and introduced them to women of color. They loved it! I recruited thirty women to join the company and, in return, the company gave me two thousand dollars in wholesale products to start my business. I was so psyched. Man, God was using me. I went to other shows where I applied makeup on people and I also sold it in the salon.

I would like to say that when you get focused on the right things you discover so much greatness inside of yourself. That is what I did over the next couple of years. Billy still worked my nerves at times but between being busy with my children and having my own hobbies and part time jobs, I hardly noticed his transgressions. They still existed, but I did my best to ignore them. I refused to allow the enemy to kill my spirit with issues that were going on in my marriage. Time marched on and my children were growing, each becoming a little more independent.

My next passion was to own my own thrift store. I loved turning people's trash into treasure. One day I was driving around city and I saw a huge thrift store that was up for rent with the option to buy. I went to my husband and told him about the idea. At first he looked at me like I was crazy and argued some points with me for a bit. Surprisingly, in the end, he said okay.

We went to the man who owned the building and put up an offer. He had other potential buyers, but God blessed us and the man took our offer. I was so excited. The store already had merchandise for sale in it so all we had to do was get our business license and complete other paper work to operate it. I was so happy that Billy had agreed with me on this business adventure. It meant a lot for him to believe in me and give me a chance to pursue my dream.

I left the hair industry for a season and went to work full time at the thrift store. I had never operated one before and there was a lot I didn't know about doing so. Fortunately, I had God and He sent a nice older lady who became a big blessing to me. One day I opened the back door to the sight of a woman with her daughter and grandson digging in the garbage behind the building. It almost startled me to death. They asked if they could take some things from the trash. I replied, "Sure".. After all, it was trash and I didn't need it. I was shocked though because I had never really seen anyone digging in the trash for things. I realized at that moment how blessed I truly was.

I felt compelled to invite them in and they offered to help me clean and organize the place. I accepted their offer and from that point on I had help. I really needed it because the place was dirty and needed renovation. Plus I was a young country gal that didn't know much about city I lived in and needed someone to watch my back. People had been coming in and stealing right under my nose due to my naivety and distraction. She became a wonderful friend. She was older than me and was a mother or aunt figure in my life. I picked her up every day for work and she was dedicated to organizing and selling the merchandise in the place. The thrift store, which l called *Metamorphosis, From Trash to Treasure*, had everything you could name in it. My new friend worked wage free, but I repaid her in other ways. I let her have whatever she needed from the store, did her hair, and took her places when she needed. We spent a lot of time together and we began sharing our life stories.

Our relationship grew until eventually God led me to talk with her about Christ. One day while we sat and talked, she gave her life over to Christ. I marveled at the Lord and what he was doing. I picked her up and took her to church with me on Sundays. The thrift store adventure lasted about six months. Then I got the great idea of turning the building into a mini mall. The building was an old grocery store so we had ample square footage. After the estimates for the conversion were finished, totaled twenty something thousand dollars. That wasn't a wise decision to make at the time on a building that we didn't even own. Eventually we stopped renting the building. The landlord let us pay our last month's rent and ended our contract.

We were thankful to God for that one. It had become very costly paying two thousand dollars a month in rent for one business, the rent at our salon, our regular mortgage, tuition for the children's private school and all the other expenses. Wow, just thinking back on all that we had going on, God had provided tremendously. One thing I would like to admit is that I have always been creative. We took chances in life starting dreams and adventures that some people wouldn't dare try. I enjoyed that.

I went back to doing hair and decided to try school again. Yes again! That time I went to Tidewater Community College for Interior Design. I realized I had a gift for beautifying things. Turning what some people might call trash into treasure was an art. School was a place for me to discover things about myself that I had forgotten I lost some parts of me when I got married but when I was at school I felt a sense of freedom and fear. God challenged me with classes that broadened my mind and helped me look forward to a new career that would enhance my life.

Thinking back to those moments, God always sent difficult professors, teachers and bosses into my life to pull the best out of me. I guess they saw something in me…potential. I personally believe everyone needs a life coach to push them to be their best. I had one particular professor, who always encouraged me. Once I had a class presentation and after I finished I gave her the material I had used. At the end of the semester she had a gift for me. I wondered what it was. When I opened the bag, it was the product I had given her from my project! She also gave me a card that read, "Thank you for your generosity and lovely gift. I think you are a creative, loving and talented lady. I'm giving this gift back as a gift of knowledge to teach you that you are enough just because. Without presents you are appreciated for yourself. I am proud to have been your teacher. All my blessings. After I read that card I felt so empowered. My self-esteem over the years had been shot. I believe God was sending people in my life to encourage me and pull me up out of my pit.

I stayed in school for a year and then I quit again because it was too hard juggling school, my children, and a stressful marriage. The marriage was hanging by only a small l limb. I remember asking my spouse what he thought and he told me he supported me but always thought I was better at being a mother. Again I decided to stop school and work on trying to restore my marriage. I put my all into restoring my house physically. I took up the f loors and pulled up the carpet on the steps, discovering real wood. I sanded the stairs and painted them with wood varnish. Upon sealing them they glowed. I was so excited. I painted all the rooms in the house and even painted the outside shutters and the front door. I planted f lowers in the grass bed outside and found a man to mow the grass. We placed grass seed in the yard and that winter my family had the greenest grass ever. It was ironic to me. My house was being transformed inside and out while my marriage continued to go down the drain.

We had an argument one Monday afternoon and I popped him in the head like you would do a child. The goal was to knock some sense in his head. Minutes prior to the hit we were in the bath conversing about his relationships with the opposite sex. I knew in my heart that he was still dealing with someone. I just wanted to hear it from his mouth. There's something about a person owning up to their sin or problem that eases the pain. In this case, we had been going back and forth for years in counseling concerning my husband and his extramarital affairs. I JUST WANTED IT TO END. I just wanted him to notice me and love me like he promised on our wedding day.

"No Kawania, I'm not messing with any woman. You know the only thing I'm dealing with is breaking all ties with the issue I'm dealing with now." he insisted." My mind raced as I thought "what do you have to break off?" Aloud I said, "Why is it so hard for you to let go?" He looked at me and asked too innocently, "What are you talking about? What do you mean?"

I was officially irritated then because Billy had decided to act dumb. I said her name but he proceeded to act like there was nothing left of that relationship. He walked out and I followed. That's when all Hell broke loose and I hit him in the head. He turned around to look at me then proceeded to leave the house. Why was he playing those games? He acted like I didn't remember catching him and her in the salon last week, chatting it up on the love seat *I* purchased to enhance the salon. In broad daylight, while clients are being serviced, my husband was at the salon with this other woman, in the establishment *we* started together. I assume he wasn't expecting me to pop up on him in hat morning since I had a hair appointment. Heck, I surprised that tail and he was caught red handed.

"Why are *you* here?" I asked Ms. Chick. She looked at me like I was in her territory or something. When she failed to respond I decided to repeat myself. I said,

"Why are you here? Don't you think you have done enough damage?" She looked at me like I was crazy or something. "Leave my salon right now; you are not welcome here", I yelled. She still didn't move, and to make matters worse, both of them just stared at me like I was the enemy. Billy didn't move either. *That really* made me angry.

I walked up close to her face and said, "Girl you know I have been praying for you. Don't you know you have caused enough drama? You had the police come to my house, arrest me and take me to jail in front of my children a week before Christmas because you were supposed to be scared for your life. Now I come to my salon and you are here when you are supposed to feel threatened by me? You have some nerve. GET OUT!" I screamed.

She still didn't move so I picked up the phone to call the police on her this time. She finally decided to make her way to the door and I helped her out. Then Mr. LOVER BOY Billy had the nerve to say, "I was doing something good." He claimed he was breaking it off; but that was a LIE. "You think my name is Stupid. You got caught once again." Then I let him have it.

"I pray for you and *this* is how you treat me? What is it about her that you can't leave alone?" He looked at me with no response. "I'm a beautiful, intelligent, creative, talented, good, and godly woman but you just keep messing me over. I'm twenty - eight years old and I refuse to be a forty year old woman... mad, angry and depressed because I stayed with a man that didn't want me. Anybody could have me, yet I choose to be here with you and this is how you treat me?" I marched out the door in despair, hurt and pain.

Four days later Billy was still acting like I'm stupid. I didn't talk to him until I called to apologize about hitting him in the head. He said it was okay, but in reality it wasn't not because that mess just couldn't continue. "Billy, you need to choose what you want. I can't make you go where I'm going and I can't promise I'm going to sit here waiting year after year for change." He just listened on the phone like he always did. "Well, are you coming home?" His answer—"No. Not right now." Seems the only time he could respond was to decline being home with his wife and children. "Okay!" I cried. I hung up, drank my tea, relaxed my mind with a song by Celine Dion called "Taking Chances", and went to bed.

God woke me at 3:54 a.m. to be exact, so I looked over on his side of the bed to find it empty. I got up and went to my daughter's room to look out of her window to see if his car was in the back yard. It was not. Then I went downstairs but he wasn't on the couch either. At that moment I knew where he was. The Holy Spirit had informed me where he was. My husband was at *her* house, not ours. I called his Mom and aunt pleading my case but that solved nothing. I ironed my children's clothes and we all got dressed. I needed to take a little road trip over by the salon to see if he was actually at her house. As I drove on the interstate, my thoughts were racing.

When I approached the exit, my stomach started to bubble from nerves. I made a right turn at the light and approached her street. I turned and drove down the street a little way. Billy's car was parked right in front of her house. I got out of the car and left the kids inside. I WAS SO ANGRY! I commenced to beating on her door. No one answered. Then I called his mother and she arrived three minutes later. We both stood outside like policemen ready to take both of them to jail. Still, no one came to the door.

Someone peeked out of the window at us, then his momma's phone rang. It was Billy alright. I was furious. I took the phone and informed him, as if he didn't already know, that his children and I were outside waiting for him. Instead of coming out to us, he had called his mother's phone. "So, I guess that means you are choosing her over us. OK AY!" I gave his mother the phone and walked back to my car in rage. I got in and took off. Mad and rejected once again, I was determined to move on with my life. I cried out to God in the car. "Lord you said you would never leave me nor forsake me." I continued to repeat the verse over and over again until I was soothed by the presence of the Lord. When I got home I went to Billy's closet and started taking all of his clothes out in order to put them in the trunk of the Volvo. I had never moved so fast in my life and it was a wonderful workout because I felt good. After that I fixed my beautiful babies breakfast. While I was doing that I called my phone company and changed my phone number. I needed to do that. It was time for a change. Then my children and I had devotions and prayed together. We all prayed for daddy. The irony was that the devotional we read was the story of Jacob and how he tricked his dad. The verses were from Genesis 27:18-19 and the moral of the story was that sometimes you may think you got away but in reality, God knows what you've done. You really haven't gotten away with anything. The person you tricked may have a hard time trusting you in the future.

Families get along best when each person is honest and kind. Isn't that how you want the rest of your family to treat you? The kids and I talked about the story and how it related to our life. My wise little daughter said, "Mommy, Daddy made a promise and he broke it. He told me he would never mess with that woman ever again and he pinky promised." Then she said, "I was reading the Bible last night and I want to read what I read to you." The scripture was in Psalms but regrettably I can't recall which verse now.

After she read, I sat at the table amazed at God and how He speaks through children. I bowed my head and I began to pray for my husband, their father. I prayed that he would decide to take the road of life and not the road of death. Then I prayed for my children's protection. Following that, I prayed for their father. Next, I took them to school and proceeded to go on with my day. I tried my best to stay focused on the things of the Lord.

Since that day I have been on an emotional roller coaster. I've done my best to stay prayed up and happy but my heart has been hurting from my experiences in this marriage. To be honest, the hurt started way before all this began. It started from that seed of rejection that I have referred to countless times in this book. When you decide to be real with yourself and can identify that you are broken, you can begin to face your issues. Then and only then can God, your Savior, proceed to save, heal and restore you. The process to healing is a hurting one because it's like this analogy that a my dear friend gave me. *"When a seed is planted in the ground, rain and sunlight give that seed its nutrients so it can begin to grow into a plant. Then, as it grows it sprouts into a beautiful flower with strong stems and lovely leaves. When the season begins to change the flower begins to transform and some of the leaves begin to die.When this process occurs it's important that you prune the flower by cutting off the old dead leaves because if you don't the dead leaves will destroy the whole flower."*

What I just explained to you is the same thing that happens to us as human beings when God is dealing with issues in our lives. There is a process for everyone on this earth and God, our Doctor, waits patiently before performing the surgery on us. When we are ready He will begin. It might hurt but the pain won't last always. Recovery begins immediately after the operation but it is up to you, the patient, how long healing will take. My question is, "Are you willing to let go of whatever is in your life that has been an idol so that God can do a work in you?" Deuteronomy 6:14 decrees, *"Do not follow other gods, the gods of the peoples around you; for the Lord your God, who is among you, is a jealous God and his anger will burn against you, and he will destroy you from the face the land. Do not test the Lord your God."* Then in Deuteronomy 7: 5-6, it decrees, *"Breakdown their altars, smash their sacred stones, cut down their Asherah poles and burn their idols in the fire. For you are a people holy to the Lord your God. The Lord your God has chosen you out of all the peoples on the face of the earth to be his people, his treasured possession."*

God believes in you. Do you believe in yourself? That was the question I had to answer. Did I know my true value and worth? Once you truly know who you are in Christ you won't settle for just anything anymore and you become the best at who God has called you to be. The Bible says in Philippians 4:13, *"I can do all things through Christ who strengthens me."*

TIME TO RELEASE

Have you ever settled for less in life, when you know that it wasn't God's best ? If so, when did you wake up? Did you learn from that experience?

_____

_____

_____

_____

_____

_____

_____

_____

_____

_____

_____

_____

_____

_____

_____

_____

NOTES

NOTES

CHAPTER 9

New Foundation

GOD WANTS TO GIVE US a new foundation, but in order for Him to do that the old foundation has to be pulled up. For example, the tree in your yard with deep roots is beginning to grow under things and take over territory. When the contractor comes to pull it up, it won't be an easy task. It is a complicated process because it disturbs the foundation. God can see the roots in our hearts, so He is gentle. God doesn't pull up the old foundation to destroy you but to lay a new foundation from new seeds. Remember the olive had to be crushed for the anointing oil to come out and the seed had to die before a plant could grow. The same process happens to us. While on earth we will face some hardships and suffering. We must learn to die daily to our flesh for the glory of the Lord. We do this so we may become like Christ on the day we see Him in Heaven and receive our Eternal Body.

Romans 5:3-6 says, "*We rejoice in our sufferings, because we know that suffering produces perseverance, perseverance, character; and character, hope. And hope does not disappoint us because God has poured out His love into our hearts by the Holy Spirit, whom he has given us.*" I LOVE this next part! You see "*at just the right time, when we were still powerless, Christ died for the ungodly.*" Very rarely will anyone die for a righteous man, though for a good man someone might possibly dare to die. God demonstrates his love for us in this; while we were sinners Christ died for us." So, folks let's get it together and realize the pain we encounter on earth doesn't last always. It makes you a better person and prepares you for your glorified body. This is not our home. Like the old folks say. "we are just passing through". Heaven is our home. John 16:33 says, "*You will face trials and tribulations but be of good cheer for God overcame this world.*"

Year 2008 I have decided to step out on faith and totally trust God. It was a struggle, but it was time for me to put my trust in the One who controls my life -- The King of Kings, the Lord of Lords, the Great I Am, Jehovah-Jireh, the Lord who provides for my life. I'd been up since four o'clock that morning when my King kissed me on my cheek and said, "Daughter get up. I wanna talk to you about some things." I got up and I started searching the Word of God for answers concerning my life. The last couple of days had been draining since the last encounter with Billy. I had been slapped in the face. It's amazing that when we put our trust in the Lord how He moves right away. Sometimes, He just waits on you to make the first move.

I had gotten involved in a prayer group called 'Vision Chaser', founded by my mentor and close friend. The group of women and men pray and fast faithfully every Monday. We go online and email each other our prayer requests. Our goal is to see the salvation of the Lord revealed in each other's lives. The previous week I had asked these men and women of God to pray for my husband, his mistress, and her children. The windows of heaven opened and released the truth, shedding light upon the situation.

That morning when God woke me up, I was determined to start moving in what I know I should do.

I just had to get confirmation through His Word. God spoke to me through Isaiah 43:18-19, *"Forget the former things; do not dwell on the past. See, I am doing a new thing! Now it springs up; do you not perceive it? I am making a way in the desert and streams in the wasteland."* Wow, those were rich and sweet words from my Lord. He loves me so much that He said, "Kawania forget about your past, baby. I got you. Don't you know I'm doing a new thing in you and for you? Kawania, I have made a new route for your journey. Girl when it seems impossible to cross over to the promise land, trust me and let me guide you down this new path."

The Word of God also says in 1 Corinthians 2:9, *"Eyes have not seen nor have ears heard the things that God has in store for you."* Then, the Lord began to speak to me more from Isaiah 54: 4-7, *"Do not be afraid; you will not suffer shame. Do not fear disgrace; you will not be humiliated. You will forget the shame of your youth and remember no more the reproach of your widowhood. For your maker is your husband. The Lord Almighty is his name; the Holy one of Israel is your Redeemer. He is called the God of all the earth. The Lord will call you back as if you were a wife deserted in spirit, a wife who married young only to be rejected, saith your God. For a brief moment I abandoned you, but with deep compassion I will bring you back."* Hallelujah!!!!

Then he took me to Isaiah 41:11-14. *"All who rage against you will surely be ashamed and disgraced. Those who oppose you will be as nothing and perish. Though you search for your enemies, you will not find them. Those who wage war against you will be as nothing at all. For I am the Lord, your God, who takes hold of your right hand and says to you, Do not fear; I will help you."* God said specifically to me, 'Do not be afraid, O little Israel, for I myself will help you'. The scripture finishes with, *"declares the Lord, your Redeemer, the Holy One of Israel."* After receiving those words from the

Lord I felt peace and hope. I knew the Lord had my back. Most of all, I knew he had a plan for my life. No, it was not over for me. A new future is beginning. Those last seven years of hell weren't in vain. God kept success on the high rise for me (this is a phrase that I learned from a dear friend). Put a book mark in it because I have to pause and give God the praise! HALLELUJAH TO THE HIGHEST!!!!!

I was raised in the country so I would like to say ya'll. Ya'll don't know what the Lord has done for me. He has set a sister free. My feet were stuck to the ground and my mind was imprisoned with fear... but God. Yes, ladies and gentlemen, sometimes we want to blame the devil for beating us up but the truth is we keep ourselves in things that God has already released us from. God had revealed to me that my former husband was having affairs. I remember waking up early one morning around 12:30 a.m. Billy wasn't home and God led me to the Bible to read a selection of scriptures concerning adultery. I did not understand at the time why I was reading it but he was revealing to me what was going on in my home. The next day I found out from the woman herself what they had done.

You're reading the book of a woman who should be dead from some type of disease, in a mental institution from nervous breakdowns, or in jail for first degree murder but God kept me. He showed me how to love through the hardest times in my life. There were times when all I could say was "Why me?" Every woman's dream is to get married and stay married to the man they love. At least that's what I wanted. I felt stuck, trapped. How would I make it on my own? How would I provide for my three beautiful kids?. I had never had the full responsibility of children AND bills. I had to pull myself together. After all, I was a strong, smart, beautiful, and talented young lady. As a hairstylist I had taken good care of myself before I met Billy. I was married now and didn't want to destroy the image we had.

What would people say though? My family, my friends, the church, what would they all say? I didn't think I would be able to live with all the questions I would have to answer. Back then I was a people pleaser and was not focused on pleasing my Abba Father. In the book of Galatians 1:15-16, Paul said, *"But when God, who set me apart from birth and called me by his grace, was pleased to reveal his Son in me so that I might preach him among the Gentiles. I did not consult any man."* This was an example of someone deciding to please God and not worry about the approval of man. Regrettably, I chose to stay in my situation for such a long time under the spirit of fear. The pain drove me to my knees. No longer would I live in bondage. I ran to God, determined not to go back. I would not look back. I repeat, no going back.

The Bible says in Ecclesiastes 3:6, there is *"A time to search and a time to give up, a time to keep and a time to throw away."* It was my time to let the marriage go and move forward with my life. God had released me. Ladies, when God tells you to do something or releases you from something then you need to move because He desires to keep you from heartache. I'm so thankful to have a God that loves me that much. I don't know what I would do without Him in my life. A friend once told me to live life with no regrets and that's what I'm doing. Let me clear some things with you. I no longer regret a thing I went through concerning my marriage and childhood. It has made me into the woman I've become today. Every detail had to take place for this book to come to pass.

This book is not meant to hurt any family member or bash my ex- husband. Every story told is from my heart and has been released for healing for my soul and for true forgiveness for those who need it. My desire is to encourage you to push through your pain and let God heal you. The Bible says in Ecclesiastes 3:7 that there is *"A time to tear and a time to mend, a time to be silent and a time to speak."*

Well, my fellow readers, for eight years I did my best to mend a broken relationship. I had been dying on the inside and destroying myself-esteem. I beat up myself because I couldn't fix things. and felt like a miserable failure. On top of that, I was soaked with rejection but addicted to fear. I was also haunted day and night by childhood memories that I had remained silent about... things that I still remember as if they just happened. Thankfully, God set me free. Like Martin Luther King Jr. said, "I'm free at last, free at last, thank God Almighty I'm free at last."

No more does shame hold me back; no more am I concerned about what people think about me. I don't care. It's time now for me to speak. Yes, to speak up with boldness and authority from God. In Isaiah 61:1- 4, God's word says, *"The Spirit of the Sovereign Lord is on me, because the Lord has anointed me to preach good news to the poor. He has sent me to bind up the brokenhearted, to proclaim freedom for the captives and release from darkness for the prisoners, to proclaim the year of the Lord's favor and the day of vengeance for God, to comfort all who mourn, and provide for those who grieve in Zion- to bestow on them a crown of beauty instead of ashes, the oil of gladness instead of mourning, and a garment of praise instead of the spirit of despair. They will be called oaks of righteousness, a planting of the Lord for the display of his splendor. They will rebuild the ancient ruins and restore the places long devastated; they will renew the ruined cities that have been devastated for generations."*

I don't claim to be some great prophet or anything. I'm simply Kawania Amina who has a story to tell about how God saved and changed me. He made me His own, took my hurts and pains, put a smile on my face and placed joy deep down on the inside of me I'm here today to share parts of my life with you in hopes of helping a change come about in your life. I desire to give you hope so that you may go and do the same for someone else.

You see, my reader, it's not about blaming someone for what you went through in life. It's about what you've learned from it. Reflect on your life. Look at the facts, admit the problem, and deal with it. Even go to the ones that may have some dealings with your issues. Most importantly, receive healing from God. Let Him heal your heart, your soul, your mind and then move forward. I forgave those that hurt me by *choosing* to let go and let God work it out. Give your issues over to the Lord. He is the Alpha and the Omega, the Beginning and the End.

Yes, He is the ruler of all mankind. He is King of Kings and Lord of Lords. The battle is not ours, it's the Lord's. Let that stuff go!!

I'm not trying to get you to deny your situation; but I am telling you it's better to ask God to help you to forgive. It's healthier for you and your body. When you hold bitterness inside of you it affects your whole body. It eats away your insides. Like a cancer that starts off as a small seed, it eventually invades the whole body until you can't function any longer. Then you will die. I personally believe the death is spiritual, emotional, or may be physical. Hebrews 12:15, Amplified Version says, *"Exercise foresight and be on the watch to look (after one another), to see that no one falls back and fails to secure God's grace (His unmerited favor and spiritual favor and spiritual blessings), in order that no root of resentment (rancor, bitterness, or hatred) shoots forth and causes trouble and bitter torment, and the many become contaminated and defiled by it."* This verse lets us know that when you allow bitterness to creep in your life, it will suck the life out of you.

In Luke 6:37-42, Jesus teaches about criticizing others. He says, *"Do not judge, and you will not be judged. Do not condemn, and you will not be condemned. Forgive, and you will be forgiven; give, and it will be given to you. A good measure, pressed down, shaken together and running over, will be poured into your lap, For with the measure you use, it will be measured to you."* He also shared this parable: *"Can a blind man lead a blind man? Will they not both fall into a pit? A student is not above his teacher, but everyone who is fully trained will be like his teacher. Why do you look at the speck of sawdust in your brother's eye and pay no attention to the plank in your own eye? How can you say to your brother, "Brother, let me take the speck out of your eye, when you yourself fail to see the plank in your own eye? You hypocrite, first take the plank out of your eye, and then you will see clearly to remove the speck from your brother's eye."*

We have no right to judge. God is the only real judge. We all have faults. No one is perfect; God alone is perfect and He is a just God. I would rather let Him take care of wrongs than for me to take matters in my own hands. Not forgiving and holding onto hate, walking through life miserable, affects everyone you come in contact with. My poison and toxic waste had been released into the airways of this world because I was hurt. I learned that hurt people hurt people I wanted to be whole, or at least on the road to wholeness through some kind of therapy. I chose to be happy and bless somebody's life rather than nurse my pain.

That's what the book of Isaiah was talking about. It was letting us know we all have been called to speak life to someone. We are then setting people free from despair, giving them hope through our testimony. Ladies and gentlemen, your life is not your own, it belongs to the Lord.

You are called to help others. Everybody on the earth has something to give to someone else. Perhaps it is just a smile or a joke for the day to encourage someone who is having a bad day. It could be buying someone lunch who didn't have any money or giving a stranger a ride to their destination. You could loan someone money who is in need, speak to your child's school for Career Day, or just volunteer in the classroom for an hour helping the teachers as needed. It could be raising money to help the poor or needy or saying a prayer for the nations. The scripture said in Isaiah 61:3. *"to bestow on them a crown of beauty instead of ashes."* The whole purpose is to make a positive change in someone else's life. We need to affect the world with so much LOVE that generations who had no hope begin to believe again, smile again, and live again. We want to see restoration of their souls.

Readers, let's not be a generation that puts band aids on our boo- boos. Let's receive the healing we need. When I get a cold I don't like taking cough syrups or antibiotics. Ok doctors, don't beat me up because I know in some an antibiotic may be needed. It's my belief, however, that if you take vitamin C and eat healthy on a regular basis you can avoid all that. I also believe in taking home remedies. I love tea. I believe green, white, Echinacea, and many more teas can keep your immune system built up to fight off the bad germs you may come in contact with on a daily basis.

The moral to all this is that what the devil means for bad in our life God turns around for our good. I hold every negative experience I went through in life to that standard. I refuse to keep blaming MAN for the way my life has turned out. It's time to turn the negative to positive. How do I do that, you ask? I keep moving forward. Don't look back. Bless those who curse you. Do well to those who spitefully use you. Life is what you make it. I'm in my right mind today. I'm blessed and I want to be a blessing. I overcame the whips and lashes of my past. I have some scars from the abuse I received. I still have f lashbacks when I see someone or something reminds me of the pain I experienced. They serve as a reminder of where I came from and how I've grown. *The devil had a plan for my life, but Jeremiah 29:11 tells me of my heavenly Father's plan: "For I know the plans I have for you, says the Lord. They are plans for good and not for disaster, to give you a future and hope."* This keeps me grounded in God so I can always be grateful for the Lord's hands on my life. If it wasn't for the Lord, where would I be? Hallelujah!!!!

Every test and trial you experience takes you to another level and glory in your life if you allow it to make you grow and not die. Learn to let go and let God have His will in your l life. Learn to say 'yes' to His will and His way. The Amplified version of Romans 5: 3-5 says, *"Moreover let us also be full of joy now! Let us exalt and triumph in our troubles and rejoice in our sufferings, knowing that pressure and affliction and hardship produce patience and unswerving endurance. And endurance, fortitude develops maturity of character, approved faith and tried integrity. And character of this sort produces the habit of joyful and confident hope of eternal salvation. Such hope never disappoints or deludes or shames us, for God's love has been poured out in our hearts through the Holy Spirit who has been given to us."* Therefore, let's 'overcome by the power of the blood of the lamb and our testimony', Revelation 12:11.

People everywhere are dealing with something. Yet I'm encouraged by the words I remember old folk used to say "Troubles don't last always." I've learned that the war I encountered is not mine alone. The Bible tells me to *"Remember that your Christian brothers and sisters all over the world are going through the same kind of suffering you are."* Satan has peeped in the future and seen some of what God is going to do with us. He tries to trick us into giving up on life and sets schemes as a bait to trap us. *1 Peter 5:8 says, "Stay alert! Watch out for your great enemy, the devil. He prowls around like a roaring lion looking for someone to devour."* My grandma was born on the same day I was. The significance of sharing her birthday is deep for me because the enemy took her out at a very early age while she was in her prime. I never met her or even saw a picture of her, but I know her story. It was full of abuse and pain. I mention this because it was the beginning of a generational cycle that I daily ask the Lord to break. She had six beautiful children that were left behind when she died, They were abandoned by their father and sent to different relatives who agreed to raise them. Then, the cycle repeated itself when my birth mother abandoned us and her nine children were scattered around. Because of this family background and the pain it caused, I was determined to break the cycle. I never wanted my children to experience any of that.

I made up my mind I would not end up like my Grandma did-- I would beat those odds. Enough is enough with the abuse of the enemy. Enough is enough with depression creeping into the lives of the women in my family... sucking the life out of us and keeping us from our purpose-filled dreams. There comes a time when a woman learns through the love of God that she has to love herself enough not to settle for less and to strive for the best.

November 16, 2008 was the beginning of my new life. On that particular day I told the devil 'No More'. I would not live in or subject my children to anymore abuse. Billy had made it clear that he was not committed to our marriage and none of my efforts to change him had worked. I got tired of changing my mind about ending the marriage because Billy seemed like he was going to do better whenever he thought I might really leave. I got tired of getting my hopes up whenever he came home early one or two nights a week (he usually came home after we had gone to bed, so the children only saw him in the mornings on the way to school). I got fed up with that. Occasionally Billy decided to spend some quality time with us, mostly to pacify me because he knew I was fed up with his junk. I got so tired of the whole mess! I decided that my children deserved better and so did I.

All those years I had thought certain things about myself and so I accepted disrespect and abuse from others. The Bible teaches a lot about our thought life. I have learned that a stronghold is nothing but a thought process. The amplified version of Proverbs 23:7 says *"For as he thinks in his heart, so is he."* I had totally lost myself. I was wasting my life. I became an emotional eater and started gaining weight. I was slowly dying. I was so fed up with the same old, same old mess. I wanted more from life. The question you might be wondering is what did it for me this time? I thought about the Cross. Jesus didn't die and shed His blood for nothing. Everything He experienced was for us so that we could have life and have it more abundantly.

Thinking about that, I had a meeting with myself in the mirror one day and said, 'NO MORE.' Like R. Kelly said, "When a woman's fed up ain't nothing you can do about it." You never realize how true a statement is until you actually experience it for yourself. I refused to think lowly of myself anymore or settle for less than God wanted for me. I ask you today, what's controlling your mind? Ladies, when you know in your heart of hearts that it is time to move on, *do it*. Don't keep doubting yourself when you have all the evidence. It is what it is. People will show you their true colors. You just have to be bold enough to accept the truth and strong enough to make the change. Know who you are. You are God's chosen child. I want to share a poem Holy Spirit gave me:

WHO ARE YOU?

Who are You? Look Inside, Deep Inside.

Do you see your soul? The threads of a woman,
a Queen sent from the King above?
That's Right Girl, Walk that Walk Girl Talk that Talk Girl !
Don't let your past label you.
Don't let the world tell you who you are.
Do you know who you are? You're God's chosen child.
You're the righteousness of his eyes. You're beautiful, intelligent and all that. Don't you know that?
NAH!
I don't think so!
'Cause you walk around with your head down singing that sob story.
But today it's GOT to DIE
because GOD'S word don't lie.
He said you were healed over 2,000 years ago.
Don't you know you're already healed?
God said you're healed ! Even when you don't feel it, you gotta believe it.
Tell the devil he's a liar;
A liar straight from the pits of hell.
Tell him who is boss.
He has no authority over you any longer. God said He already won the battle for you. So press GIRL, press
YES, I said press!
Don't you lay in the bed another day and let your purpose go by the wayside. God needs you.
Yes, GIRL, Didn't you know it? HE loves you!
He wants a relationship with you. That's why that man will never
satisfy you because God, the Alpha and Omega,
the Lover of your soul is
the only True Man of your life. The Husband of all WOMAN Kind ! Know who you are!
Be who you are! WALK That WALK GIRL! TALK That TALK GIRL!
That's right, I dare you to heal; I dare you to heal.
You are healed.
Don't let the devil feed you lies.
He's the liar. You're the winner.
That's right because God's the Healer, the Healer of all mankind.
He is the King of Kings and the Lord of Lords, the ruler of all mankind.

by Kawania Amina Brickhouse

That November morning I calmly but firmly announced that I wanted a divorce. There was no more double mindedness. **I was done**. James 1:6 says, "…*he who doubts is like a wave of the sea, blown and tossed by the wind. That a man should not think he will receive anything from the Lord; he is a double- minded man, unstable in all he does.*"

Billy knew we had come to the end of the road. He released me without a fight. YES!!!!!!!!!!! I felt like a heavy load had been taken off me. I never thought I would escape the fear of the unknown due to my lack of confidence, but God gave me the courage I needed to do what I had to do. Thank God He never stops loving me and I never stop calling on His name.

Life is what we make it. Moving on with my life was the best decision I had made in a long time and I have been experiencing so much freedom ever since then. I'm like a butterfly, a bird, a bee. Ladies, I'm *free*. I was in a cage that seemed to be beautiful. I was content in that cage because I had some of things there that I loved. Later I realized there was so much more I needed to experience outside of my cage. "Just go outside that window" was spoken over me at my church by a man and his wife who prophesied over me. I was a little confused at first because I didn't understand it's meaning. There were a lot of major decisions I needed to make, so I received the word. As time went on, God allowed the story to unfold with the help of an obedient spirit (mine). I just stepped out in faith. The Bible says in Hebrews 11:1, *"Faith is the evidence of things hoped for, not seen."* In life you have to step out on faith sometimes, even when you can't see the final results. Something inside of you says 'go for it'. That's the Holy Spirit giving you revelation on what to do next.

How many women can relate to what I just said? If that spoke to your soul then it's time baby, it's time. Don't sit there another day and continue to abort your dream or the destiny that God has for you all because of fear. The devil is a liar. He can't have you any longer. Believe in the God in you. Know this right now. You can't do it without God.

You need God, the Author of your book, to be by your side. He wrote the story. Trust in Him. He has your back. He had and still has mine. My life is a living testimony. I would not be here in my right state of mind today, writing this book, if the Lord wasn't the ruler of my life. The Bible says in Proverbs 3:5 to '*trust in the Lord and lean not unto your own understanding but in all your ways acknowledge Him and He will direct your path*".

TIME TO RELEASE

What has to die in your life in order for the birthing of a new life or new season? In other words what do you need to let go of? Whether it's a person, place or habit that means you no good?

_____

_____

_____

_____

_____

_____

_____

_____

_____

_____

_____

_____

_____

_____

_____

NOTES

Now that you released your thoughts. Embrace my painting called "Surrender". That was me surrendering years back. I pray you choose to always surrender your will so you may fulfill your life purpose.

CHAPTER 10

Faith shattered!,,, but God!!!

I'M A WOMAN OF FAITH and back in the day I used to speak life over every situation that came my way. I even spoke life over my dear friends and family. It didn't matter what the problem was, I would say, "What does God's word say about this?" I always pleaded the Blood over the storms that came my way and even anointed that person, place or thing. I just believed God could fix, heal and do anything!!!

Well, after my divorce I was jacked up! The enemy came at me full force and stole my ex-husband away. My faith was shattered. I was weak and vulnerable and didn't know how to go on. There were days I didn't want to even get out of the bed. I thought life was over for my three musketeers and me. To be frank with you, I never wanted a divorce. I didn't believe in it, but some things God will remove from your life for your own protection or because it's not part of His plan for your life. Even so, I struggled with feelings of failure and unbelief. Why couldn't I speak life over my situation? Why was all my hope gone?

How is it that when we get hit in the core areas of our lives we get weak and ready to give up on life itself? I've learned from a study I did in the book of John that only when you enter your wound will you discover your glory. Where a man's wound is so is his genius. The wound is located at a place of your strength and is targeted by the enemy in an effort to take you out. Until you go back to that wound, you are still not living to your potential. From your brokenness you will discover what you have to offer to the community. When you begin to offer not just your gifts but your true self, that's when you are ready for battle!!!

After that great attack on my marriage, my true battle began because the next attack was on my top priorities -- Love and Family. My core foundation had been corrupted from birth by my biological parents. They planted seeds of rejection and abandonment in my spirit. It became my battle ground because that's where the enemy tried to take me out. However, my spirit also became a place of victory, not just for me but for God's Kingdom! It is where I decided to go to war and do damage for the Kingdom. Although the spirit is a sensitive place, it's a place of Grace and Glory; a place where God brings the former and the latter together for His Glory. It's a place He wants to fill with freedom and peace. When you decide to let go of the hurt, you can declare that what the devil meant for your bad you are going to use for your good. He tried to kill me in this area but I'm setting souls free.

Readers, I say to you when obstacles come and old memories surface in your mind, don't ignore them -- expose and deal with them! Speak over the situation. Life and death is in the power of our WORDS!!!! Let them free you and help someone else!! You are an overcomer through the power of Christ!!! Romans 8:35-37 says, *"Who shall separate us from the love of Christ? Shall trouble or hardship or persecution or famine or nakedness or danger or sword? As it is written: 'For your sake we face death allday long; we are considered as sheep to be slaughtered'. No, in all these things we are more than conquerors through HIM who loved US!"* Those things may have tried to kill you but look in the mirror today. They didn't! You're still here!!! You're alive and God wants to make you whole and fill you with His spirit. Look to GOD!!!!!!!!!!!! The devil didn't win then and he will not win now! Whatever obstacles come your way, know it's just a test dressed up in a new costume!! LOL!!!! The Devil has already been defeated!!!!! Tell yourself that. Yell it from the rooftop!!!!!!! Speak life into *every* area of your life!

TIME TO RELEASE

Have you ever felt like you were stuck in limbo, in your life? Not knowing what to do next, but you knew there was more to your story. If so, release where you feel stuck and write out what could be the ending of your story? In the bible the book of Habakkuk 2:2 it reads "And the Lord answered me, and said, Write the vision, and make it plain upon tables, that he may run that readeth it." This verse is letting you know that if you have a vision or idea. Write it out and present it to the Lord. I encourage you let loose with your pen.

_____

_____

_____

_____

_____

_____

_____

_____

_____

_____

_____

_____

_____

_____

NOTES

_____

_____

_____

_____

_____

_____

_____

_____

_____

_____

_____

_____

_____

_____

_____

_____

_____

NOTES

CHAPTER 11
No Looking Back

WHEN IT'S TIME TO MOVE forward, no matter where you are, you gotta do it. God will call all of us at a particular time to surrender our will to Him, the King of Kings and Lord of Lords. I declare and decree I will not look back at my past. I am a new creation in Christ today. Old things have passed away and all things have become new. My past is my past and I declare Philippians 3:12-14, *"But I press on to possess that perfection for which Christ Jesus first possessed me. No, dear brothers and sisters, I have not achieved it but I focus on this one thing: Forgetting the past and looking forward to what lies ahead. I press on to reach the end of the race and receive the heavenly prize for which God, through Christ Jesus, is calling us."*

God, I was thinking about what I went through next and I am going to be honest. I am ashamed about what I am going to share. I wonder what the readers, will think. Will they not think I am a Christian or true woman of God because of my actions? More than anything I know I am, regardless of my past. It's amazing to witness about Your forgiveness! As a Christian, what keeps people bound is their shame and the condemnation from what others say. Who can put me in a heaven or hell but You my Savior? Well, let me just put it out there.

Still hurting from the divorce and wanting to move on, I got in a relationship with a guy. We talked for a while but I put off spending real intimate time with him. I didn't want to put myself in that predicament. I knew I was vulnerable. There were still things in me I wanted to free myself of. One of those things was the desire to be with a man, just to feel complete. I was 'thirsty' though. We began spending time together, becoming acquainted. We kissed and messed around a little but never went too far. One night Billy had the kids, so I invited the guy to my home. Everything felt so right and eventually we started making out, which led to us having relations. *One* encounter and I got pregnant!

Fear ran through me. *Uncontrollable fear.* I felt I had to do whatever I could to fix the situation. How could I deal with my family and friends? What would I say? I was divorced and already trying to take care of three children on my own. It was my desire to have more children someday, but not out of wedlock! Not again. Not me, not Kawania! I didn't want to do it,but what did I do? I did what the flesh wanted. I was selfish and destroyed God's creation by means of an abortion. I don't think I was even eight weeks pregnant, maybe six. Since I was so early, it was not a major surgical procedure, just a pill and a suppository. Then it was done. I was set free. *I thought.* After taking the prescribed actions, I thought my world would return to normal. It didn't. I would always have to live with that memory.

God is forgiving and, yes, He did forgive me. I begged for forgiveness even when I knew what I was doing. It was premeditated. I did that. I murdered God's child... handsome son or a beautiful daughter. Why, when I had so much love for the ones I already have? I was so scared of what people would think.

Ladies, I want to share this with you, men as well, that no matter how hard the situation or sin you are struggling with, it's important to have a confidante to encourage, push, and show you the right path. These people keep you from journeying down the wrong road. If you make the wrong choice, God's grace is sufficient to forgive. When you repent (admit you were wrong), He wipes away the sin and takes away the guilt. It's gone, like a new cleaned plate. You are free, no more walking in bondage, fear or doubt. You just have to believe it and move on. I know it's easier said than done. I fought hard to forgive myself. Though I have moved forward, there have been some 'woulda - coulda - shoulda' thoughts. I even struggled with adding this experience in the book, but I believe God wants me to always be transparent.

The counseling for sexual wholeness I received from the program I was involved in the past. There was a man that was a Christian but he had to contend with deviant sexual behaviors. He battled with the thought that he was abnormal but his transparency set the standard for helping others to heal. We have all fallen short of God's glory, but we can be set free from the shame and delivered *if* we will be transparent. The root of my situation was not the abortion; it was what caused me to have it in the first place. Why was I single and still having sex? Why did I give myself to a man that I had not married? Yes, the act felt good, but the truth of the matter is that I did not need to be doing it. I longed to be held by a man and wanted love and affirmation, so I did what I was not supposed to do. I knew it was not right, and I paid the consequence by getting pregnant.

I had tried to cover it up, but God spoke to me. "Kawania, here it is. You are divorced and you have had sex with more than one man. Look at the repercussions. Here you are crying and upset. What you seek is not in a man, but in Me. You need a love that only comes from Me." Ladies, you can sleep with many but they will never satisfy you. The Bible said that Jesus asked the woman at the well where was her husband. She told him that she was not married. He said 'yes, you have been married five times' (John 4). The point is that she had gone from man to man. What she sought and longed for was not with the men. Her dream was not in a husband or a relationship but a commitment with the Father.

I've discovered that God is my daddy. I had looked for love in all the wrong places, from a child to a teenager and onto an adult. I have been married and divorced and found myself dating again. Still no love found. The kind of love I want comes from my daddy above. I remember the day I laid on the couch crying out to God, crying out for freedom. I thought I needed a man to fill the void inside me, to feel secure and complete. I was married for nine long years, but I never felt secure or at peace. There was no completion. My ex could not make me feel complete. The only one who can is God, my King, my Lord and Savior, the Lover of my soul, and Forgiver of my sins. He wipes every tear and restores my soul. He is my redeemer who bought me at a price when He died on the cross that I might have life and have it more abundantly.

I don't know how you see me at this point. Do you want to call me a hypocrite? Call me what you want. I know who I am. I am Kawania Amina... a queen with a plan and a vision; a queen with a great future. I made a great mistake, but I am grateful that my Daddy forgave me and revealed the truth to me. I don't want to point fingers or blame anyone else. I realize the true root to this madness. I am getting the help that I need. I am glad I now know where my affirmation comes from. No longer do I need to define myself by being with a man. I believe God will give me another husband one day but that man won't define me. God defines me. I am His daughter, His child.

Whatever your struggle, whatever your sin, you don't want to share, know that you can share it with Him. Someone out there can sympathize, empathize, pray and encourage you. They can lead you to the well where you can receive your healing. They can pray you through whatever situation. You don't have to share it with the world, but if he speaks to you I encourage you to do so. I can't explain the freedom I'm receiving from being transparent. Our past is a pool, a bridge to discipleship which takes footholds from the enemy. It frees us and others. Walk in liberty as He designed.

Luke 22:20-34 tells us that during His last supper, Jesus stood and declared that He would be betrayed. Simon (Peter) swore he would never be the one to do it. He professed Jesus as the Son of God and in response to this declaration, Jesus renamed him Cephas (Peter in Greek). Simon means 'small stone or pebble' but Cephas means 'rock', like a boulder. What is a rock? It's something strong and hard. Isn't that amazing? Jesus knew Peter would betray Him and He still gave him that name. Jesus saw Peter as his already glorified self. He doesn't see you just as your sins. He sees you as you will be. He forgives even when he knows what you will do in sin. That blows me away! If he could forgive Peter who denied him when he walked with him, He can and will forgive you. I would like to pray at this time because that was something crucial that I just shared.

I pray in the name of Jesus, that You Father in heaven, will come right now and move upon the hearts of every reader. Send the Holy Spirit to reign over your people, the just and the unjust, that their lives will be changed for your glory. I pray for Christians who want to live a godly life but fall and don't know how to get up. I pray for their strength to look You in the face and say 'I need your help to move on'. May they confess their sins to you right now as they read this book. I want them to know that your word says You forgive and cleanse because your grace is sufficient. Right now, wherever they are, meet with them. Your love is raining on them, washing them, and making them whole; for all those who are lost and need Christ. I ask that you repeat this next sentence.

I pray in Jesus' name for forgiveness. I believe in you, Jesus. I believe that you are the Son of God and that you died on the cross for our sins and rose to give us eternal life. I want to live for you all the days of my life. Father, I am saved and I am redeemed as your child. I am thankful that you are moving tremendously in the lives of all who are reading this book. I pray it will be like a bombshell that explodes and newness will take place... a fresh new start. I would like to say congratulations to those who are believers and have already confessed their sins. God loves you and so do I. In Jesus's name I pray, Amen.

When you're going forward with your life, the process can be a challenging one. You find yourself thinking of old thoughts from your past, allowing memories to haunt you. TD Jakes said it well in a sermon to singles called 'the Art of Forgiveness.' In this process God is teaching me to truly give past hurts over to Him and to pray for those that have harmed me. That's really the only way to move forward. Learn to bless those who wronged you and continue to forgive them. That is how you release them and yourself. You have to do it over and over again until finally the offense doesn't bother you anymore.

I had to go back to God numerous times with past issues from my former marriage. Why? I was picking up old ghosts here and there in my thoughts, rehearsing the pain... pain that I needed to leave in the grave. It seemed that the pain kept following me. There

I was in the prime of my life and certain things were still bothering me because they were constantly in my face, which really wasn't healthy for me. For example, Mr. Ex and his girlfriend, the same mistress he had when I was married to him, moved to the area I lived in. Her children and mine were attending the same schools. It was a bit too much to digest. I thought I had broken free from all the mess after the divorce but it seemed she was back in my circle again! I didn't want to be a big Brady Bunch family. I wanted freedom from all the madness and drama., but there was something God seemed to want from me... FORGIVENESS. I needed to forgive my ex-husband's mistress!

Some things you just can't run from. I don't care what state or country you move to, if you have bitterness in your heart it will manifest itself until it is dealt with. I say to you, my sister or brother, "Don't run; stand still and go through your surgery so that after the procedure is done, it's really done. True healing only comes from forgiving.

God was on my back about getting my issues in check, so I made the decision to befriend what the world would call my enemy. Really, what could I lose by being kind to someone? Besides, my children cared for that woman. It wasn't easy, but it did happen. I did forgive her. The Holy One living inside of me released me to move the way I did. I also believe that when you put your feelings aside and think the way God wants you to think, you can see the root of a thing. God let me see that I'm not perfect. He also wanted me to know that it's only by His grace and mercy that I hadn't done to someone else's marriage what was done to mine.

I know some of you reading this book are probably thinking I'm crazy, but, oh well, I don't care. I know for a fact that if God can set me free from unforgiveness. He will do the same for you. The key is allowing Him to have His perfect way in your life. I hear the cry for revenge from some that are reading this book. NO! NO! NO! NO! NO! But God is the avenger. He says in his word, Romans 8:18-21, *"If it is possible, as far as it depends on you, live at peace with everyone. Do not take revenge, my friends, but leave room for God's wrath, for it is written:*

'It is mine to avenge; I will repay" says the Lord. On the contrary: if your enemy is hungry, feed him; if he is thirsty, give him something to drink. In doing this, you will heap burning coals on his head. Do not be overcome by evil, but overcome evil with good." These verses are powerful. The reality of the verse really comes from ancient Egypt's custom of having people that felt bad carry a pan on their head with hot coals in it as act of repentance (Romans 12:20, *Life Application Study Bible* foot notes).

Sometimes it doesn't feel normal doing things for those that have harmed you, but you have to do what's right, not what feels good. Our feelings are unstable. We are emotional but we can't live by our emotions. In the process of forgiving your enemy, if you don't know what to say just do what's right. It will lead toward a healthy outcome. One good deed can outweigh bad thoughts and darkness. In my case, I called the woman and told her that I forgave her for the past. I also let her know that I appreciated her being there for my children when they spent time with Billy at her house. My comments led to a fresh start for the both of us.

I would like to say it's better and healthier to make an enemy a friend than to carry hurt, bitterness, rage and pain inside of you. Forgiveness leads to longevity, wholeness, peace, and richness from Christ above.

Hate, however, leads to sickness and death and I don't want that. Do you? With that being said, why is it that we talk about certain things that can profit us nothing but pain? My past was just that but every blue moon I allowed my f lesh, as well as the enemy, to remind me of things that don't mean anything anymore.. Those past things did hurt me once, but they won't rob me of my future. I have a new vision and new dreams. My future looks bright, beautiful, and prosperous. The truth is now that I've accepted myself, everything I ever wanted to do is coming to pass.

You see, I used to hate who I was and didn't want to live because of my circumstances. What a waste of life if I had given up! One early morning, the Holy Spirit spoke to me through His word and said through Isaiah 54: 4-7 *"Do not be afraid; you will not suffer shame. Do not fear disgrace: you will not be humiliated. You will forget the shame of your youth and remember no more the reproach of your widowhood. For your Maker is your husband. The Lord Almighty is His name. The Holy One of Israel is your Redeemer, he is called the God of all the earth. The Lord will call you back as if you were a wife deserted and distressed in spirit, a wife who married young, only to be rejected" says your God. For a brief moment I abandoned you, but with deep compassion I will bring you back."* When God said that to me I cried like a baby; it was a cry of relief, a cry of healing, a cry of wonder. WOW, I thought, God understands me. He hears me. He feels my pain. He knows the truth and He won't leave me. I'm not alone.

Let me share a WORD OF ENCOUR AGEMENT at this point:

➤ To everyone who's reading this book, God hasn't forgotten about you. Do you hear me? He has been with you through the whole process of your life. Every hill, valley, and bridge you have crossed, He was carrying you.

➤ To the person who has lost a loved one, He is there for you. Share your heart with Him. He wants to minister to your soul and revive every weak place.

➤ To the person who's divorced, He will restore every hurt place inside of you if you allow him and if you desire to get married again then He will bless you with your heart's desire. Trust Him, God is not a man that He should lie.

➤ To the person who wants to take his own life, I say NO!. STOP right now and choose to *live*. Your life matters; your voice counts. You can make a difference in this world. Don't you give up… Keep Moving… Keep Striving… Don't look back… The past is behind you.

I want to share a set of scriptures that has allowed me to move forward and finish this book after many years of it sitting on hold. The day God gave me these verses, I was feeling real low. I remember laying in bed in the middle of the day with the bedroom curtains closed. My head was buried in the pillow and I hoped life would just end for me. I tossed and turned, trying to sleep my life away, but I couldn't sleep. Frustrated and depressed, I sat up and began to cry. After all I had been through, I felt life was worthless and I didn't have the energy to keep moving forward. I needed help. I wanted someone to empathize with me. I was having a gigantic pity party but God wasn't having it. He kept tugging at my spirit. He wanted me to be strong and put my boxing gloves on. It's alright to cry, but afterward you have to get up and keep moving. God let me know that I had to put my combat boots on and fight the good fight of faith. It was time for me to become the cheerleader I never became in high school, lol……. HA HA HA HA!!!!!!

I remember pulling my Bible out and opening to Isaiah 45. The tears rolled as I read. I got out of the bed and went to the mirror. I looked a mess. I dabbed at my face and went back to the bed and continued to read the verses. The more I read, the more my inner me began to rise… The Holy One was telling me it was my time: *"This is what the Lord says to his anointed, to Cryus (I put my name there) whose right hand I take hold of to subdue nations before him and strip kings of their armor, to open doors before him so that gates will not be shut: I will go before you and will level the mountains. I will break down gates of bronze and cut through bars of iron. I will give you the treasure of darkness, riches stored in secret places, so that you may know that I am the Lord, the God of Israel, who summons you by name. For the sake of Jacob my servant of Israel my chosen, I summon you by name and bestow on you a title of honor, though you do not acknowledge me. I am the Lord, and there is no other, apart from me there is no God. I will strengthen you, though you have not acknowledged me, so that from the rising of the sun to the place of its setting men may know there is none besides me. I am the Lord, and there is no other. I form the light and the darkness, I bring prosperity and create disaster, I the Lord do all things. You heavens above, rain down righteousness, let the clouds shower it down. Let the earth open wide, let salvation spring up, let righteousness grow with it; I, the Lord have created it.*

Woe to him who quarrels with his maker, to him who is but a (potsherd) among the (potsherd) on the ground. Does the clay say the potter, 'What are you making? Does your work say he has no hands'? Woe to him who says to his father, 'What have you begotten? or to his mother, 'What have you brought to birth?' This is what the Lord says, the Holy One of Israel, and its Maker: Concerning things to come, do you question me about my children, or give me orders about the work of my hands? It is I who made the earth and create mankind upon it. My own hands stretched out the heavens; I will raise up Cyrus in my righteousness: I will make all his (her) ways straight.

He will rebuild my city and set my exiles free, but not for a price or reward, says the Lord Almighty. This is what the Lord says: The product of Egypt and the merchandise of Cush and those tall Sabeans- they will come over to you and will be yours; they will trudge behind you coming over to you in chains. They will bow down before you and plead with you, saying Surely God is with you and there is no other god."

After reading that powerful word I was encouraged. I had hope and knew that God was keeping me alive for a purpose; my life was not going to be thrown by wayside. There was destiny inside of me that needed to come forth. Who was I to disagree with my Creator and the reason He birthed me into this world? He made me and designed every part of my being just the way He wanted. Once I got this in my spirit, my whole outlook changed. My vacation of pity parties, depression, stress and anxiety was over. I had to go to war for my life and my children's. I was Kawania, His anointed Woman of God... A Queen. I had a lot to live up to. No throwing in the towel for me. I'm a warrior! I decided to always put my best foot forward in everything. That's why I'm now so passionate about life, people, family, and my God.

I no longer question God about why He made me the way He did. I take my time working on the clients that sit in my chair to get their hair done or their makeup applied for a special event. I was put on this earth to help women realize who they are and discover the queenship inside of them. I'm here to encourage all people and to help them see the good in any situtaion. This is Who I am, a woman of honesty, integrity and faith. I am focused and I am determined to keep moving toward my destiny. One of my destiny achievers has been to publish this book and although it took a long time, thank God I finally listened to my accountability partner and completed it and there's more books to come. Procrastination for five years have kept this book from being published, but thank God I'm free from that negative characteristic now. I'm accepting nothing, but best for my life.

I say to women, as well as men, who have been broken, hurt and confused, want to curse the day they were born, but you can't. You are here on this earth for a reason. I dare you to be all God created you to be. I dare you to get BOLD and BAD for the Lord.. Yes, do it for Him. No more laying in the bed letting your dreams go by the wayside. Say what Dr. Martin Luther King said all those years ago….. I HAVE A DREAM!!!

I heard someone once say that "to give up on your goals is like committing spiritual suicide." After I heard those words I had chills go all through my body. Im going to vow to God and myself and to readers that are reading this book that I will commit myself to never giving up on my goals and dreams that has been placed inside of me.

I pray you walk out your dream no matter how hard the road ahead becomes and allow the obstacles to shape you into being the best you! I ask you to vow to never give up on your goals and dreams and lastly I ask to read this last poem, its about believing in ourselves and not giving up. I pray it encourages you as much as it did me:

FEAR IS NOT ALLOWED

Fear, Fear,
You can't have me anymore.
Fear, I said you can't have me anymore.
You had me just too long.
Fear, I have to say Goodbye to you.
You tried to destroy my life; You tried to kill me.
Even in my mother's womb you were after me.
You were after my life.
Fear, I said you can't have me any longer.
Fear, You've had too many people; You have destroyed too many lives;
You are not allowed in my life any longer.
I won't allow you to keep me in prison any longer.
Fear, what did I say? Get away from me and Never come back.
Fear, you're not allowed in my life any longer.
No matter how hard the struggle is, No matter how hard you try.
You cannot have me any longer.
You lived in my mind,
You tried to take over my body.
You lived all around me.
Hiding in closets, hiding behind doors, even hiding behind the front
door I needed to walk out of. But Fear I say to you today
I declare to you. You can't have me. I stand up to you
I look you straight in the eyes. Go back to the pits of hell,
pits of darkness where you belong. Because fear you can't have me, any longer. WHY?
Why can't you have me? Because I'm the righteousness of God.
He woke me up this morning and put breathe in my body.
He gave me legs to walk with.
The sky was shining; it was bright and blue.
I turned over:
my sons and daughters was there too.
Fear, I said you are not allowed in my life any longer.

No matter what you say No matter what you tell me It's over!

It's not comforting being in your presence any longer.

No!

I said No, it's not! You're just an imagination! You're just a feeling!

And

You're not even real.

You destroyed so many people's lives.

You killed so many others.

But you won't kill me and you won't kill my family.

You can't have me.

I will live.

I will be the woman of God He has called me to be.

I will walk the walk.

I will walk with my head up high.

My back arched and breast plate of righteousness setting out; yes, I will.

Fear you can't have me any longer. Yes, I said you can't have me any longer No matter how hard you try.

I'm saying GOODBYE, TODAY.

Yes goodbye!

Why?

Fear, I said goodbye! See ya later, alligator!

Remember that. After while crocodile.

Oops! There's no after while. Because I'll never see you after while. I'm moving on with my life.

I'm walking the walk! I will talk the talk.

I'm going on with the life God has called me to fulfill.

Full of Joy, Peace, and Happiness that only comes from HIM.

Why?

Because I have joy deep down inside.

Why?

Because my Lord reigns in my life.

Why?

Because God is who He says HE is.
That's why!
He is the Alpha and the Omega The beginning and the end. He's the first and the last
And my very best friend.
That's Why!
That's why you can't have me any longer.
Today is a new day,
a day of new beginnings.
A day of dreams coming to pass in my life.
Yes, dreams I said.
Yes, today is the day that I will walk.
I will walk!
I will face you, Fear!

You can't have me any longer, No matter what you say.
No matter how tempting you are.
I will not lay in that bed any longer; I will not cry those tears any longer.
I will move on.
Because Fear you can't have me any longer!
I say Goodbye! I say farewell!
I say Hallelujah!
No, you can't have me any longer.
Thank you God! I'm free from fear.

-Written by Kawania Amina Brickhouse

TIME TO RELEASE

Now that you have completed my book Who are you? I hope and pray that it has encouraged you to go deeper with you own life. My purpose for sharing my story, was the hopes of you taking a look at your story about who you are. Defining and dealing with hard memories from your past, so you can properly move forward with your destiny. No matter what stage you are in. We all have a opportunity to discover something new about ourselves, because we all are growing and evolving in this life in every season young or old. Now one of my last assignment I have for you. Involves you pulling out some magazines, scissors, makers, colored pencils, glue stick and putting on your thinking cap once again. Come on!!!!!!! This will be fun. On the next page I have a work sheet for you the reader. If you're a male I need you to design your King if you're a female I need you to design your Queen. After writing this book God told me, my mission for life was three letters EIC, thats Elevate Inspire and Create. My mission is to elevate you to the next level, so you are inspired to create your own world. With that being said. I have drawn out a silhouette of Queen and King. If you don't already know it. You know it now. You are royalty. That is the Foundation of who you are. I have a quick question for you. In chapter one of this book you learned that 1Peter 2:9 says what?

_____

_____

_____

_____

Hopefully you wrote the right answer down. God chose you my King or Queen. He loved you so much he made you and inheritance of ROYALTY… You have his BLOOD running down through your veins. YOU are co heirs with CHRIST. That is enough right there to go running. My next question for you. What's is the definition of Purpose?

_____

_____

_____

_____

Google dictionary defines it as: the reason for which something is done or created or which something exists.

So, my next question. Why where you created? What is your reason for existence. Now if you didn't know. We all were created to worship the LORD and bring glory to His name. What s your specific task the Lord has given you? Think about. Your not just here for a purpose, but you literally purpose. Describe your purpose. Write it out. And then draw it out. That's why I have blank King or Queen on the next page. So you can have a small goal board designed by your hands with all the intimate, creative details of who you are and your specific task that you have complete for God, for yourself, your family, for the world around you. Remember people are waiting on you. Your special assignment is meant to help bring change to this big world in some special way. My last verse for you to mediate on is 1 Corinthians12:12 "There is one body, but it has many parts. But all its many parts make up one body".…. If you keep reading in chapter 12 from verse 12 through 27 it will break down in depth. The importance of everyone having a specific function and one part of the body can't work without the other part. It's truly a powerful message. I encourage you to study that chapter. My purpose for sharing this with you. Is to help you understand. You have to discover who you are. Which I believe by this time a huge light bulb is going off in your mind and heart and GOD is revealing great thing to you and only you. Also you have to fulfill your purpose by accompanying me on this journey and designing your ROYAL QUEEN or KING. I promise you it will bless your life.

NOTES

_____

_____

_____

_____

_____

_____

_____

_____

_____

_____

NOTES

Now just a few more instructions. Use the extra note paper to take you some notes about your purpose. Write what comes to your mind, whether its dreams and goals from child hood, or new ideas that just surfaced. Just start releasing. Next I want you to write down the colors you see in your mind, after you finish writing out your purpose. Finally I want you to go to work. Just start. Whether you write words in the inside of royal silhouette or draw out visuals with bright colors or cut out things that represent who you are and what you will do. Just start creating... I would love to be there to see your final results. I know its going to be amazing. If you want to send me a copy of your final project. Take a picture of it and email it to me. I would love to pray for you and your journey.

NOTES

NOTES

NOTES

Now my last question I leave you with once again.

Who Are YOU?

Now go make a difference in this big world.

Be Blessed and remember fear can't have you!

Printed in the United States
By Bookmasters